PLAY ON YOUR HARP

MEDITATIONS ON BIBLICAL THEMES

ROY A. HARRISVILLE

AUGSBURG PUBLISHING HOUSE
Minneapolis, Minnesota

TO MY MOTHER

PLAY ON YOUR HARP

Copyright © 1975 Augsburg Publishing House

Library of Congress Catalog Card No. 74-14188

International Standard Book No. 0-8066-1471-4

Scripture quotations unless otherwise noted are from the Revised Standard Version of the Bible, copyright 1946, 1952, and 1971 by the Division of Christian Education of the National Council of Churches.

Manufactured in the United States of America

Contents

Preface

Preaching is never a light or easy thing. Now that I've been cooped up in an academic institution for a decade and a half, pulpiteering's become more arduous for me than ever, and particularly in the presence of students! Only a handful of these talks were delivered outside the chapel at Luther Theological Seminary, St. Paul, Minnesota—across the "puddle," at a former parish or in my home congregation. Such a restriction may, perhaps, limit their applicability. But, dear reader, if you can enjoy or use these paltry things, and in whatever fashion you choose, they'll have done some service.

My thanks to Christine Miller for preparing the typescript.

Roy A. Harrisville

A Look-See

(Communion)

> So when the woman saw that the tree was good for food, and that it was a delight to the eyes, and that the tree was to be desired to make one wise, she took of its fruit and ate; and she also gave some to her husband, and he ate. Then the eyes of both were opened, and they knew that they were naked. (Genesis 3:6-7a)

> When he was at table with them, he took the bread and blessed, and broke it, and gave it to them. And their eyes were opened, and they recognized him. (Luke 24:30-31a)

When a man chooses to know the secret, the mystery of Being or what-have-you, when he elects a sight of the truth of it all *on his own terms, in his own good time,* the best he gets is a peek into the anthropological situation. That's what the story in Genesis three is all about. After entertaining the notion of setting the knowledge of good and evil by their own watch, and letting that notion bird-like build a nest in their hair; after that delicious hemming and hawing makes playing with temptation such delight, and that final resolution to experiment, to touch, to taste, and all on their own say-so—after all that, Mr. and Mrs. Adam got only a sight of themselves without britches. That wasn't what they were after, of course—they wanted to be like God! And all they got was a lesson in anatomy. Ever since, to mix the metaphor, man's been pulling the lever on some celestial slot-machine

and getting a handful of air, and teasing himself into loving it
in the bargain.

Now we're *made* to touch and taste and see, to discover and
explore and learn and grow. And the current assumption that
any ass can paint by hurling pigment at a canvas, or write poetry
by tossing words at a page without giving himself to the rigor of
stretching his mind with mastering a few of the rudiments, will
pass with all those guitar lessons by correspondence. God speed
the day!

It's all a question of when and where and who—when will
you touch, and where will you taste and who will make you
see? Faith is after bigger game than a course in anthropology.
It's after a sight of him, a look at God, if you please! That makes
faith a waiting game, a hard-nosed refusal to enter the bargain
basement and come away with stuff that'll never suit its yearning! Faith must see God, not its own reflection. So it leaves the
when and where to him, refusing to pick its own occasion. It
won't touch where others touch or taste where others do. It won't
see where others see—it'd rather be sightless, like a child at a
party, blindfold, trying to pin the tail on the donkey while land-
ing on its head behind the sofa—not for the sake of its cynicism
or even the mystic's vision, but because it throbs with a hope
that won't be stilled till the One who put it there sets that hope
to rest in the sight of him!

Now right here's the time and place to touch and taste and
see—right here! And you didn't plan it, you didn't get it up.
Oh, you fussed with it some, as anyone but the most superficially
acquainted with the history of liturgical theology can plainly
see. No matter—you're like the two at Emmaus now. The time
is his; the bread and wine are his; the blessing is his and the
handling and eating, the seeing are his gift. What you eat and
drink and see now won't be much, but it'll be what the old

King James calls an "earnest." It'll be a pledge, a promise—
enough to keep the old hope and yearning burning, enough to
make you critical of Kant's critique or Hegel's theodicy or John
Q. Public's homespun or Barth's theology or the rest of us! It'll
be enough to make you want to wait with all that's in you
when the rest have run pell-mell to the mirror on the wall; it'll
be enough to fill you with a yearning that will nearly burst your
whole insides! You weren't made to die like Narcissus by the
reflecting pool, you see; you were made for the sight of God!

So eat and wait, drink and hope. Deny what others affirm,
spurn what others touch, be blind to what others can see—like
him, like Jesus on his cross! Someday you'll see, and that sight
will be more than fair trade for the pain of not knowing, not
really knowing good from bad, not being like God, not having
the secret to Being or what-have-you. It'll be more. I can sense
it, like an arrow ready to leave the bow can sense its mark.
It'll be more!

Play on Your Harp

Now the Spirit of the Lord departed from Saul, and an evil spirit from the Lord tormented him. And Saul's servants said to him, "Behold now, an evil spirit from God is tormenting you. Let our lord now command your servants, who are before you, to seek out a man who is skilful in playing the lyre; and when the evil spirit from God is upon you, he will play it, and you will be well." So Saul said to his servants, "Provide for me a man who can play well, and bring him to me." One of the young men answered, "Behold, I have seen a son of Jesse the Bethlehemite, who is skilful in playing, a man of valor, a man of war, prudent in speech, and a man of good presence; and the Lord is with him." Therefore Saul sent messengers to Jesse, and said, "Send me David your son, who is with the sheep." And Jesse took an ass laden with bread, and a skin of wine and a kid, and sent them by David his son to Saul. And David came to Saul, and entered his service. And Saul loved him greatly, and he became his armor-bearer. And Saul sent to Jesse, saying, "Let David remain in my service, for he has found favor in my sight." And whenever the evil spirit from God was upon Saul, David took the lyre and played it with his hand; so Saul was refreshed, and was well, and the evil spirit departed from him. (1 Samuel 16:14-23)

Some Englishman who thought he knew something about it said that "music hath charms to soothe the savage breast, to soften rocks, or bend a knotted oak." He should have added that "music well played, or played by someone who knows how hath charms, etcetera." Fellows like these have aided and abetted all those doting parents who send their darlings off to music

9

lessons and increase the pain and anguish of the race. Let's first
make one thing perfectly clear—to quote one currently unem-
ployed pianist whose repertoire extends only to "happy birthday
to you"—this story in Samuel is not meant to encourage all and
sundry to "take up" the "cornet, flute, harp, sackbut, psaltery,
dulcimer, and all kinds of musick."

But the story does have something to say about excellence.
David was "skilful" at harping, or whatever you call it. He had
"know-how" as the Greek Bible suggests, and whenever he took
to the lyre, King Saul was refreshed and the demon left him.
Now, from this we oughtn't to conclude that the acquisition of
skills will eradicate evil from the face of the earth—no matter
how attractive that notion might be. It's skill or excellence in
a certain kind of person that makes him a good match for the
savage mood. Whoever referred that boy to the king, after list-
ing the qualities which normally fill any letter of recommenda-
tion—"a man of valor, a man of war, prudent in speech, and a
man of good presence"—he noted, and almost incidentally, that
the Lord was with him! What Saul needed was someone in the
grip of God with a little know-how, someone in the hand of the
Almighty who was handy with the harp. Later on, little David
would prove himself expert with the slingshot as well. Amaz-
ingly talented, that boy! Armed with five stones, he'd take on
Goliath whose spear was as big as a weaver's beam and shout
across the valley of Elah: "You come to me with a sword and
with a spear and with a javelin; but I come to you in the name
of the Lord of hosts, the God of the armies of Israel, and this day
the Lord will deliver you into my hand!" And one stone was all
it took! That boy on whom the Spirit of God fell "mightily,"
as the Good Book says, that boy had know-how!

And you don't, is that the problem? You're not adept at anything, so abandon excellence, grab a gimmick on the run and

play the rest by ear, right? Chin up, little David, the very same God has made you his, *and* in such fashion as David never could have been, man or boy. You're the man David hankered after being—a king and priest forever! "The Spirit and the gifts are ours," not for a moment, as they were for Saul, but for keeps! You're anointed; you're a pneumatic, a charismatic. You're the new man, plunged with him into his death and raised with him to new life, and what's left is merely to decide on the bassoon or piccolo—or exegesis, perhaps, or history, or systematics, or homiletics—and then stick at it so as to achieve a bit of expertise!

Someone's in a savage mood, someone's in the thrall of some demon, and he'll not get well with a tyro. It's those everlasting beginners hammering away at the keys like smiths at their anvils no doubt drove him crazy in the first place!

He needs, he wants the music of God's amazing love in Christ played by a man who knows how. Luther once said that theology without *Wissenschaft,* without science, was the root of all evil, and Paul had something of the same in mind when he urged all those beautiful saints in Philippi to *think,* to think on whatever is true and honorable and just and pure and lovely and gracious. Now, you've got the Spirit—how about a little *Wissenschaft?* Not for yourself, bless my soul, but for him, for that Saul. Develop a little know-how, a bit of skill, and maybe you'll free someone of his dark shadow! And if not, there's still Another, that One who matters more than any other, waiting to shout: "Encore! Encore! Play it again, Sam!"

Thanks!

(Communion)

Offer unto God thanksgiving; and pay thy vows unto the
Most High. (Psalm 50:14)

In the worship of the old church, after the catechumens and
the penitents had been dismissed and the Mass of the Faithful
had begun, the people came forward to the altar, bringing gifts
of bread and wine for the communion. From this ancient custom we derive that part of our worship called the Offertory, a
portion which in our own time has degenerated into a mere
"taking up" of the collection, or into an organ recital designed
to spare Christian people the pain of hearing the footfalls of
their neighbors who turn their backs on the sacrament in favor
of an early lunch. In other words, for the old church, the com-
municant's appropriate act, his appropriate response to Christ's
rendezvous with him at the altar was sacrifice, a sacrifice sym-
bolized by the gifts of bread and wine. And we know of what
sort that sacrifice was. In a little document of the second century
called the *Didache* or *Teaching of the Twelve Apostles,* Christians are admonished to pray as follows in connection with the
cup: "We thank you, our Father, for the holy vine of David,
your child, which you have revealed through Jesus, your child.
To you be glory forever"; and, in connection with the bread:
"We thank you, our Father, for the life and knowledge which

you have revealed through Jesus, your child. To you be glory forever. As this piece was scattered over the hills and then was brought together and made one, so let your Church be brought together from the ends of the earth into your kingdom. For yours is the glory and the power through Jesus Christ forever." In a time when the Lord's Supper was still a real supper, when believers still looked hotly and expectantly to that day when the Messiah would drink new wine with them in his kingdom, they offered the sacrifice of thanksgiving. The communion was really a Eucharist then.

That note of thanksgiving is strangely absent in the Supper now. Some prefer to find the explanation for its absence in the fact that that hot, joyful anticipation could not hold out against the Lord's perennial delay. It was because Jesus did not come that the believer was compelled to look back with brooding on his death rather than forward with thanksgiving to his return. But that explanation does not satisfy me. There are places enough in Scripture to indicate that that very delay was regarded as cause for rejoicing; not least by Paul, and even after he had allegedly "given up" the idea of Christ's speedy return.

No, there is a better explanation, and it lies in the nature of man himself. For if a true thanksgiving is at once the recognition of a void and a surrender to whatever or whomever can fill it, or, as Luther comments on this psalm, the confession of having received everything from God and the sudden sacrifice of oneself to him with the whole heart, then that is precisely what men, even religious men, even Christian men, prefer not to give —not even in the Supper!

That isn't to say that we no longer bring our gifts to the Supper; that the element of sacrifice has disappeared; that we no longer need the Offertory. There are still gifts a-plenty! We bring our piety, or better, our sobriety. We ascend the altar stairs with it so carefully, like little children playing the game of carrying beans on a knife—one smile, one exultant twinkle, one kind greeting, and the spell is broken, the gift is lost, the rendezvous is off. Yes, the Lord's Supper is a solemn event indeed, but laughter, laughter that rises from having marked the infinite, impossible difference between myself and the God who descends to me here is infinitely more appropriate to the occasion than sobriety. And, we bring our contrition here, or rather, our attrition, for a contrite man brings with him a resolve, but we come merely with a tabulation of old, repeated faults—for that is much easier than to resolve, to surrender totally to the Power that frees men from such slavery

But God will not have such sacrifices. Not that God spurns piety or sobriety or attrition—but they are not an appropriate response to what he is doing with us here, or, for that matter, anywhere. These sacrifices still leave a part of me to myself, a little citadel from behind which I can protect myself against being altogether overwhelmed by God.

"But he is truly worthy and well-prepared who believes these words: 'Given and shed for you for the remission of sins.'" That is, he is truly worthy and well-prepared who is thankful, for thankfulness, the thankfulness appropriate to this rendezvous, involves the same recognition and surrender which are implicit in a true faith. It alone lets God be what he is, lets him do what he will with us.

So, dear friends, if we cannot offer what we must, if we cannot give that which God most of all desires, then let us admit we have nothing with which to come to this altar, and then, while we wait for it, while we long for it, while we pray for it, he will give us what we need to answer him: thankful hearts! Then we shall really make our sacrifice!

Revive Us Again!

Wilt thou not revive us again, that thy people may rejoice in thee? (Psalm 85:6)

When I read that story of the coming of the Spirit in Acts, about those people on whom their God fell, it's like reading about something which occurred on another planet. Like a fire gotten out of hand their gospel scorched the earth. When I read the story of the Apostle, driven beyond endurance, turning prisons into pulpits and printing presses, stoned, sick, and half-dead most of the time but all of the time galvanized by an all-consuming power which never left him, from which he never found rest nor wanted to till it was kicked out of him somewhere in Rome in A.D. 68—it's like reading about a creature from another world. There was an abnormal, driven, compulsive something about all of them made them say and do and endure what scarcely another class of beings has ever said or done or endured. I'm tempted to disbelieve the story, to ask "Can it be true? Did such people really exist?"

There is a powerful difference between them and us. If they were the fellowship of the possessed, then we're the fellowship of the well-integrated. There's no madness, if you know what I mean. And there isn't the red-hot climate to produce it. We've bought a thermostat to preserve ourselves from the extreme temperatures which make for such complete abandonment to a cause. We need a new hymn-book right enough, a medium-warm hymnbook with stanzas like this:

Like a mighty tortoise Moves the Church of God:
Brothers, we are treading, Where we always trod.

Sleeping in the morning, sleeping through the crises,
Sleeping in the noontide and the dewy eve.
Waiting for the harvest and the time of reaping,
We shall come sedately, bringing up the rear.

The results have been commensurate. Once, societies, empires, whole cultures were torn down to make room for others. Cynical, against his will, Edward Gibbon admitted in his *Decline and Fall* that "a pure and humble religion gently insinuated itself into the minds of men, grew up in silence and obscurity, derived new vigor from opposition, and finally erected the triumphant banner of the Cross on the ruins of the Capitol." Perhaps the judgment on our little fellowship will be that we struck a bargain with our world, agreed to retreat from it, to leave it to itself; holed up in our caves, hermit-like, to escape contamination. It is a question whether that sedate and sterile structure we call our church will do for ours what that fellowship in Acts did for its own century.

And this is a century which needs a bit of doing for! For it's one great, hell of an age which encourages man to affirm, accept and choose only his death as the pre-eminent possibility of his life. What needs to occur to offer men hope? Revival! Revival begun at the house of God. This moderate, medium-warm organization of the Golden Mean needs to be possessed again! As on that day, to the accompaniment of cloven tongues of fire and an eighty-mile-an-hour wind God fell on those who yielded to him, driving them to demolish the world into which they'd been born and to hammer up another. Revival is the thing!

Now if someone had popped into that Pentecost parlor and asked what they were all doing there, they would have said:

"we're waiting, and we're hoping." This may seem a poor bit of advice for us who do little enough for our time. But it happens to be one of the ironies of God that when men resist the impulse to be up and doing just for up-and-doing's sake, he begins his mighty work.

How long is it since you've stopped moving about long enough to pray to God to descend on you? How long since you've been possessed with the idea of a life, a community, a world, brought into subjection to the will of Christ? It's been a long, long time, hasn't it? But if you aim to squeeze and knead your world into something resembling the shape its Creator intended it to take, you must first be struck mad! First kneel and pray: "Lord! Revive us again!" Then go build your new world!

Jonah

> When God saw what they did, how they turned from their
> evil way, God repented of the evil which he had said he
> would do to them; and he did not do it. But it displeased
> Jonah exceedingly, and he was angry. And he prayed to
> the Lord and said, "I pray thee, Lord, is not this what I
> said when I was yet in my country? That is why I made
> haste to flee to Tarshish; for I knew that thou art a gracious
> God and merciful, slow to anger, and abounding in stead-
> fast love, and repentest of evil." (Jonah 3:10-4:2).

When the word of the Lord came to Jonah, son of Amittai,
he didn't stand there, like Moses, fishing for compliments: "I'm
really not leadership quality, and what's more, I flunked public
speaking." Or all trembly like Isaiah: "Woe is me! I'm undone!" And he sure'd never hankered after a revelation, like
Habakkuk. When the word came, he lit out for the coast like
a cat with a tin can tied to its tail, bought a one-way on the first
scow to Spain, tumbled down below decks, and sat there behind
a barrel of kippered herring, shivering and chewing his nails.
Because he *knew* what would happen. Jonah knew! And when
he was finally bludgeoned, battered and badgered into doing
what he'd tried like fury to avoid, he said: "I knew it! I knew
it all the time! I knew you were gracious and merciful, slow to
anger, and abounding in steadfast love! So I preached and the
people repented and you took it all back and I'm out of a job,
mucking around in a pile of useless posters and throw-aways,
with a whale of a printing bill!"

But he couldn't escape him, Jonah couldn't. God hurled a

wind, shivered the timbers like Moby Dick shook the Pequod, threw the crew into a horror, got his man tossed into the drink, used him like a wriggling worm for bait, plunged him into the belly of Sheol where he yelled, "How shall I again look upon thy holy temple?", had him vomited up on the shore, all slimy like a child fresh from the womb, and said: "Arise, and go to Nineveh!"

Another God wouldn't have bothered. Or he'd have wrecked that city in some grand, Olympian fit of passion as Zeus wrecked Troy, and then let Jonah do a jig around the rubble, cackling and whistling over the cosmic ruin. But this God would rather not be without his Nineveh. He'd rather not be if there weren't someone to love and love him back again. He'd rather dry up or evaporate or disappear, cease to exist, if there were no man he could father, no woman he could be husband to, no crying child he could soothe. And Jonah had made himself a victim, a casualty of that unrelenting, implacable, sovereign love. That's what this little book's all about—God's love, love in hot pursuit of a mouth to tell it, love putting the screws to a man wouldn't make it known, an inexorable love, looking for a whole city to flood with light and joy!

If there's a moral for you and me in this ancient, little piece, it's that you and I are nothing, and they're everything—those cities out there. Whatever in the world we're doing here, it's all for those God has his eye on, his mind on, his heart on.

For he's a lover, that One, and not in business for raising up prophets to "trouble Israel" and there's an end to it. He's in a hot sweat for the whole world to embrace, aching to warm it like some giant, celestial hen; in an anguish to give it life and set it free! And if you don't believe me, turn the old book to pages further on and watch the most amazing reversal of roles in all the world, signalled in that cryptic word: "This generation seeks a sign, but no sign shall be given to it except the sign of Jonah." He turned Jonah, he did, and let Nineveh, let the city play God. He thought to flee and trapped, nailed, wrote his own lyrics to Jonah's tune: "I am cast out from thy presence . . . the waters closed in over me, the deep was round about me; weeds were wrapped about my head at the roots of the mountains. I went down to the land whose bars closed upon me for ever!" He turned Jonah—omniscience, omnipotence, holiness and the great "I am" turned ignorance, weakness, sin and a nobody, got itself hurled and tossed, sunk in deep darkness and spat out —in Jesus, Jonah from Nazareth.

The little book ends with a question, with nary a word about the prophet. Did he stay there, under the withered plant, and die of his integrity? Or did he give in, consent to that remorseless, unpitying love he always knew was there but ran from, then live to sing it?

And you, you who were made for that love and have a mouth to tell it—will you die for *your* integrity, or, will you let that love of his hew the harness of your own brand of "prophetic truth" from you piece by piece till naked you wait its stroke? *You* finish the book—but one thing you've got to know. You'll never see, never hear, never taste another love like this. By the hand and eye and tongue and heart of God, you'll never know another love like this, come down at last, turned Jonah, in Jesus from Nazareth.

Tomorrow

Now when John heard in prison about the deeds of the Christ, he sent word by his disciples and said to him, "Are you he who is to come, or shall we look for another?" And Jesus answered them, "Go and tell John what you hear and see: the blind receive their sight and the lame walk, lepers are cleansed and the deaf hear, and the dead are raised up, and the poor have good news preached to them. And blessed is he who takes no offense at me." (Matthew 11:2-6)

One thing you'll have to give the Baptist. He could put a question straight out. "Are you he who is to come?" Not a single fringe, frill or firbelo to that question. It's like a bald head—naked. Naked of any politeness, for one thing. I'd have begun "Good morning Jesus, Sir; it's a beautiful day; do you think the rain'll get the rhubarb? Now something's been nagging me, and I hope you won't be offended, good gracious, no; I've never been one for rhetoric, but are you, are you . . ." and then let him finish my question for me. You might say I've been "programmed" to broach such delicate things with "preliminaries," with the sort of polite fandango two cocks go through before the feathers fly. This quality, this handling of questions as though they were clubs for cracking skulls is what many youth have in common with the Baptist—it makes every day a fray for the likes of me. I ask myself: "Where have all the amenities gone?" and turn in nights feeling as though I've been invaded, my psyche exposed, my identity threatened, my wisdom challenged, my information faulted. Pitiful. But he never minded. He was never one for the amenities. He couldn't be, for he often

21

dealt in the same brash coin. One night, in a ruler's house, while the guests were all hopping about the table looking for their place cards, he viciously attacked them for scrambling for the best seats, and not content with that one monstrous breech of decorum proceeded to instruct the host in table manners: "When you give a dinner, do not invite your friends, invite the poor, the maimed, the lame, the blind. . . ." He had "cheek," Jesus did, a kind of cosmic "cheek," and he took no umbrage at a like quality in John.

There's more—John's question contained the suggestion that if Jesus wasn't the One, he, John, wasn't about to put all his eggs in *that* basket, wasn't about to bet all his money on *that* horse. He'd begin to look elsewhere, for an alternative. He came flat out and said "or shall we look for another," meaning, "however comfy-cozy skooting and skedaddling around with you and your friends may be, if you're not the One, then I'm out for bigger game!" The Rich Young Ruler had at least the decency, the *savoir faire,* as the French say, to keep his mouth shut and just walk away "sorrowful." But the Baptist had no manners—if I'd been Jesus, I'd have felt as I did when some callow youth button-holed me and said "I'd considered coming to the seminary, but I've heard such negative reports from juniors about curriculum and about the faculty's squeezing everybody into the same, tra-ditional, parish-pastor mould that I'm thinking now of going to Harvard!" Harvard indeed! For all of me he can go where the pepper grows! But Jesus didn't mind. He even went so far as to allow *he* might be an offense to John. He reserved a benediction for him provided John didn't stumble at what he said and did: "Blessed is he who takes no offense at me."

Somewhere, on every page of the Gospels, there's an example or two of that kind of "reverse English." A man asks "who's my neighbor?" and Jesus turns the question 'round to read "to whom can I be a neighbor?" Someone invites him to a party and he turns out to be the host. Pilate tells him to open his mouth and say something—his life is in his hands—and all of a sudden Pilate is fumbling around as though *he* were on trial. And here, to John's impropriety, Jesus suggests that the offense may really be with *him!* It wasn't that he was making allowances for John—John, poor John, rotting in prison, John, about to lose his head to the establishment, John, loaded like a Napoleon with the ball and shot of apocalyptic yearning, hoping, dreaming, straining, bleeding, his belly sour-sweet with honey and grass-hoppers, skin all sore from camel's hide and voice like raw beef-steak with yelling "you brood of vipers!" and all of that, so that the poor blighter needed humoring—it was "reverse English," to begin with.

Sometimes I wish I could furnish you who are troubled with John's question the evidence, the unambiguous, unequivocal evidence that all the goodness, truth, light and freedom men can conceive or haven't yet dreamed of has dawned in that carpenter from Nazareth. (That would really make me king of the hill, wouldn't it?) But I can't. And it's not just that I'm ig-norant, that whenever my poor logic bursts its seams I can only bleat out something about faith. Part of the reason lies in the this-or-that-and-who-knows-which-way about things. Jesus said: "Go and tell John what you hear and see: the blind receive their sight and the lame walk, lepers are cleansed and the deaf hear, and the dead are raised up, and the poor have good news preached to them." But it wasn't only Jesus who did such things, at least to the mind of his contemporaries. There's enough in Virgil's *Eclogues* or Apuleius' *Golden Ass* to convince us be-lief in such goings-on was a common-place. Not even Jesus' bitterest enemies doubted his power—the only question was, did it come from God or from the lord of the dungheap? Men were just as hungry for evidence then as now, and the evidence was just as ambiguous then as now.

But the best, the juiciest reason why I can't do what I sometimes want to do is that what Jesus brings is a tomorrow thing and tomorrow can only be entered with hope. It's tomorrow that makes logic burst its seams. It's tomorrow that forces logic to say "if, if, provided, assuming, granting that the world goes on as it has, then such and such will occur." But tomorrow can't be entered with qualifications and assumptions and ifs and provided thats, at least not the tomorrow I'm thinking of—hope, expectation, anticipation, vision is the proper posture for that tomorrow. It's not that human reason can't do a bit of anticipating—but what it anticipates is always built on what happened yesterday. But what if tomorrow should bring surprises! What if it should bring an end to the perpetual round of hate and disease and blood and death? An end to the old and a new thing, an unbelievably new thing signaled, not proved, not guaranteed, but signaled in the healing of a blind Bartimaeus, the cripple by the pool of Siloam and the raising of the widow of Nain's son?

It's that tomorrow that renders the evidence ambiguous. For if all the evidence were in, tomorrow would already be here—and what would there be left to hope for? But if there is nothing to hope for, then there is no use to being a man, for that is what man is, a creature, a thing of hope, bones and sinews and viscera all sewn together by hope. If man is not that, if hope does not drive him, give his faith its shape and command his love, man is nothing and nothingness his only alternative. Mere fear is no reason for keeping alive. No one understood it better than Matthew—not even Paul. The tomorrow toward which the ancient prophet strained had only dawned in Jesus, had only begun, the sun had only begun to rise. There was more to the

prophet's dreaming than that handful of words Jesus quoted to
John: "the blind receive their sight, the lame walk, the lepers
are cleansed, the deaf hear, the dead are raised up." There was
more, a whole heaven and earth more: "Waters shall break
forth in the wilderness, and streams in the desert; the burning
sand shall become a pool, and the thirsty ground springs of
water; the haunt of jackals shall become a swamp, the grass
shall become reeds and rushes. And a highway shall be there
. . . the redeemed shall walk there . . . everlasting joy shall be
upon their heads; they shall obtain joy and gladness, and sorrow
and sighing shall flee away." That's for tomorrow, that's tomorrow's surprise! That's for hoping!

And then, Jesus said something about John has nothing to
do with "reverse English." A pity old Bultmann dismisses that
word as a mere appendage. No matter—anywhere else you
look in Matthew, you find Jesus saying "yes" to John—echoing
John's word, building on John's work, gathering John's disciples for his own, maybe even following as John's disciple
before beginning his work, planting John in the tomorrow, giving him a share in the surprise. "This is he," Jesus said, "this
is he of whom it is written, 'Behold I send my messenger before thy face, who shall prepare thy way before thee.'" And
why? Why did Jesus do that? Because what John preached,
what John demanded is the twin of hope. There's no kingdom
without hope, there's no tomorrow without hope, there's no
being a man without hope, but there's also no kingdom and
no tomorrow and no being a man without radical transforma-
tion of the self, without recognition of the difference between
myself and the God who brings tomorrow and its surprise,
without repentance! And there, there is where the ordinary,
run-of-the-mill world-beater, world-changer, whether to left or
right, shatters and breaks apart. There's where a reactionary shat-

ters, two steps away from fascism and burned books and people squashed like rotten apples. And there's where an activist shatters, captive, sucked in by an idealism which screams hate for the sake of some love-abstraction. How are they different, apart from their point of view? Polarize the masses, and what's left— the same man, all spleen and gorge and four letter words at either pole. A new man is what tomorrow requires. Not prejudices rearranged—scorn for Bach where there was once scorn for hard rock, and scorn for hard rock where there was once scorn for Bach; anger and passion and bitterness on behalf of change where there was once anger and passion and bitterness on behalf of the status quo; hate for the left where there was once hate for the right and hate for the right where there was once hate for the left—a new man, without scorn, anger, passion, bitterness and hate, with nothing left but hope, faith, and love; a new man born from above, not an alteration of opinion; a man born again, not a man like you and me, but the man we were made to be. We will destroy the earth and one another— we have already begun—right wing, left wing and silent majority —unless, until that new man is born.

And he's born, that new man's begun where Matthew began, simply, with hearing the little word that concludes the chapter of our text: "Come to me, all who labor and are heavy laden, and I will give you rest. Take my yoke upon you, and learn from me; for I am gentle and lowly in heart, and you will find rest for your souls. For my yoke is easy, and my burden is light." Hearing that little word—that's where he's born, that's how the kingdom's gained, that's where tomorrow begins!

Humanity

(Communion)

Jesus took bread, and blessed, and broke it, and gave it to
the disciples and said, "Take, eat; this is my body." And he
took a cup, and when he had given thanks he gave it to
them, saying, "Drink of it, all of you." (Matthew 26:26b-27)

That giant of humane letters, Johann Wolfgang Goethe, once
dubbed humanity "the only fortune of earth and the only true
theology." Now, suppose we didn't know what that word "humanity" meant. Suppose, with all the exhorting and editorial-
izing and the heaping up of volumes on the subject of being
human, we didn't have a clue to what human being is, had no
proper definition of it? Or, assuming we had such, suppose
being "called to be human"—the title of a Sunday school book
of recent memory—were a call to something to which we couldn't
respond, a command to perform an impossible thing like riding
'round the moon on a broomstick?

Call me animal, vegetable, mineral or all three at once, and
summon me to animal behavior, to walk erect and on my two
feet like a proper bi-ped of the genus homo; summon me to
vegetate—I know something about that! But what is it to be
human? Can you tell me? Two hundred years ago, folks said,
"it's a thought, it's thinking that makes a human being; ratioci-
nation's the thing to distinguish us from the rest of what is."
Dictionaries still describe us as differing from other things by

our "extraordinary mental development." A century ago, folks said, "feeling is of the essence of the human, and of the divine, for all of that." Fifty years ago they said, "decide! decision's the thing to make us human," and now here we are, back to feeling again. There are a million people on this polluted planet calling me to be a human being, each with his own definition, each ordering me to fit my existence to it, and once in a while wreaking some terrible havoc. "Deciders," say, are still trying to live down their association with a monster whom Martin Heidegger heralded as "the man of unprecedented resolve."

Sometimes I'm as confused as that fellow in Abner Dean's cartoon. The whole world, the entire cosmos is in total ruin, and this naked, scrawny thing clambers up the highest hill, raises a megaphone to his lips and yells: "Will the three wise men please step forward!"

So what's human, wise men? But while I'm asking, something else is rolling around in my head—those words: "This is my body, this is my blood." Could there be a connection between those two things, between those few, little words and my question? Might they perhaps shed a bit of light? What if, what if humanity or being human is at bottom a secret, a mystery a man has got to be let in on, not something he has with simply leaving the womb or can summon up at the count of three? What if none of us is human till Someone gives us our humanity or, better yet, shares his own with us? "This is my body, this is my blood." We're always and forever bothering our heads with how Deity can communicate itself through such rude objects as bread and wine, but what if man, not God only, but man, woman, humanity, is given here, in things like these, at a place and time like this? What if only one man has ever stood upon the earth, the rest of us all the while living a shadowy existence like those figures in Plato's allegory of the cave, at least until we heed his word to "take and eat, this is my body, and this is my blood"?

The Psalmist wrote, "what is man that thou art mindful of him?" and took the definition of "man" for granted. He didn't know what he was doing, but when Pilate stood on that pavement and shouted to those holiday crowds, "Behold, the Man!" he helped me and thousands like me to a notion of humanity. Jesus Christ! That's man, and God into the bargain! Jesus Christ! That's humanity's secret and Deity's mystery unlocked and exposed, here for the getting, for the eating and drinking. Come now, be a man! Be a woman! "Take, eat," it's his body, his blood, his life, life of the one God and the one man, "the only fortune of earth and the only true theology."

Follow!

(A Sermon to New Students)

> And passing along by the Sea of Galilee, he saw Simon and
> Andrew the brother of Simon casting a net in the sea; for
> they were fishermen. And Jesus said to them, "Follow me
> and I will make you become fishers of men." And imme-
> diately they left their nets and followed him. (Mark 1:16-18)

There's a suddenness to this event that makes the head swim.
Jesus suddenly summons those two to follow, and they just as
suddenly respond. The whole scene, of course, lacks what the
mini-Freuds call "motivation," psychological preparation. And,
to the utter despair of generations of parsons who love to regale
their audiences with a million and one fictional accounts of how
Peter and Andrew got to the point where they were convinced
Jesus was worth running after; of how they cogitated and rumi-
nated and chewed cud on the question of Messiah's coming—
oh, friends! how they cogitated!—of how their suspicion began
to grow that Jesus and messiahship were somehow tied together;
how they studied the alternatives, interviewed other candidates
for the job, and then, finally, one day by the sunny shores of
Galilee, brought all that cogitating and ruminating and what-
not to a head by ditching their boats to follow him.

Mark, who obviously didn't care a fig for such clap-trap, had
something else in mind. He had it in mind to tell us that Jesus'
call and the answer of those two fishermen had something of

30

the quality of the first creation about it. "And God said, 'Let there be light'; and there was light." Now light didn't tarry about, didn't consult Henry Kissinger before it emerged. It had no option but to shine, then and there. "And immediately they left their nets and followed him"—it was something like the first creation. Those two had little choice but to leave their boats, just as that Communist fellow in the Italian version of Matthew's Gospel filmed it.

There's a lesson here somewhere for you, with your college diploma all bright and shiny. You're entering now upon the study of theology, that queen of the sciences turned Cinderella, and you may be counting on your pursuit of her to lead you to a kind of certainty you've not yet got. Or, you may have decided that praying professionally, while it'll never make you rich, will at least keep you in meat and potatoes—and that's a guarantee two thirds of the world's population can't claim. Or, abysmally inept at anything else, you may have determined that chancel prancing and pulpit pounding are an art which can be mastered with a minimum of skill and intelligence. Whatever your reasons—good or bad—there's someone summoning you now, and he'll not wait about for you to debate his credentials or his authority. He made the world, he led the children through the sea, carried them back from exile, healed the sick, raised the dead, set us all free, and by his cross made sure that power would never again reside in kings and tyrants and prime ministers and presidents and bishops but in submission and death. "Follow me!" he says.

Peter and Andrew had no time—or if they did, it was of no interest to Mark—no time to ask where Jesus was going. Anyone in his right mind would ask "where to?" "Where to, George, where to, whatever your name is?" Open any college catalog—"this institution aims to prepare young men and women

to blah, blah, blah." And we once had a catalog here whose
stated aims and purposes rivalled the phone-book. It just wouldn't
do to have folks running about aimlessly, would it? A man's got
to have goals, right? Plastics, maybe! And, I'll wager, some of
you are already setting up goals—the parish, perhaps, that is, if
the church turns out to be something other than some Brob-
dingnagian thing intent on squashing your tender little self like
an overripe tomato. Or, teaching perhaps—a good salary and a
sabbatical leave every seventh year. You can just see yourself
now, standing regal before a crowd of avid, hungry listeners,
squeezing out that abstruse, theological stuff like shiny pearls
on all those happy, happy heads. Goals is what a man needs—to
think, succeed, be a proper fellow, make a mark in the world.
"Where to?" A terribly important question, that question of
goals. But those two, Peter and Andrew I mean, never asked it.
At the greatest moment of their lives, when it came to abandoning everything they'd ever been or done; when it came to jetti-
soning everything they'd ever loved and worked their fingers
to the bone for, they never asked "where to?" Incredible!

So the question of means never got asked, either. For if they
never bothered to ask "where to?" they obviously didn't think
to ask how in the world they were going to get wherever in
the world they were going. Ordinarily, folks who don't consider
goals and means are folks who've had lobotomies. I don't know
if the world could last one minute if someone somewhere weren't
reflecting on goals and means; I don't know if we could even
think, eat or sleep, allow for our natural, vital, functions, without sometime or other giving attention to goals and means. Yet,
when Jesus Christ called Simon and his brother to follow by that
Galilean shore, they never asked where to or how. Somehow
that summons blocked out thoughts and imaginings which normally fill a man's head, and they left whatever former existence

they'd enjoyed just for the sake of following him! That was certainly not a reasoned response as we imagine it. It was more like an obsession, a possession. They were suddenly possessed by Jesus. It was like the creation story all over again.

There's Someone standing here, the sight of whom is glorious and magnificent enough to make you forget what men normally bother about, and whose summons is somehow strong enough to lift you above or set you beneath all that, Someone whose very self can become to you a goal, an end and a way—"I am the way, the truth and the life," he said!—Someone who sums up in his own life and his own word everything which normal men normally associate with aims and means, and infinitely more, because to see him, hear him, follow him, love him is not merely to have your life enhanced, improved, embellished or what have you, but to have it transfigured, without resemblance to what it once was—a transfiguration, a renovation as total and complete as though come from nothing. Like the first creation.

Now, you may decide to fret and fuss about what you're going to do with your life, and how you're going to do it. You may get to turning your hair grey with such questions, and spend most of your days trying to adjust your goals to your capacities and choosing between better and lesser means, and in the end take your place with that vast company of the grey middle in the church who've traded one spontaneous "yes!" to the King of Kings and Lord of Lords for a life-time of monotonous management. But if there's one of you for whom Jesus Christ will be enough, mind you, he's not calling you to just anything at all; he's not summoning you to "identity"—"to thine own self be true," and all that sort of thing. He's calling you to himself. And answering that summons will mean a kind of death. Death to your own values, wherever in the wide world you got them, death to your self, to its sensuality, death to the ego, to the passions and a life absorbed, swallowed up by him.

It doesn't matter, in this moment at least, whether or not you want to be a pastor. Chances are, you'll end up just another functionary, praying for pay. There are more preachers in hell than in heaven at any rate, as John Chrysostom said. It doesn't matter, in this second, whether or not you want to be a teacher or a bishop in the church, obscenely exhibiting your Ph.D. in public, frightening little children away from whatever they learned in Sunday school. But would you like, would you entertain the notion of, would you perhaps warm to the idea of becoming a disciple, a disciple of Jesus Christ, letting him fill your whole soul to the point where you don't give a continental for things men fuss about, where there's light and fire and love, bless my soul! love so pure and complete you'll need no other? No? Then what in God's name are you doing here? Yes? Then it'll mean a death for you, and I doubt the death will be neat and clean. Most likely it'll be a slowly grinding wheel. But sudden or slow, it'll be a dying, and that'll be hard, with your fresh, young ego, just hankering to burst out of its cocoon and play God Almighty.

Perhaps you're wobbling between the yes and no. Are you wobbling? You see the disparity between yourself, your existence and all those beautiful people in the New Testament, and don't dare call yourself a disciple. Yet, in some quiet moment, unexpected, off-hand, you hear him summon you, through a long-neglected and suddenly remembered verse, from the stanza of a tattered old hymn like "Amazing Grace," and you've a yearning in you so great it's like a horror which blots out everything else under the sun, when talk of goals and means and projects and plans and everything else in the universe somehow disappears in face of that longing. In that moment, Jesus Christ, son of Mary, dead and risen, spells meaning, glory, beauty, power, infinite love, love without strings, without conditions; spells the beginning and the end of everything and everyone; means yesterday, today and tomorrow, wife, children, mother, father, uncles and aunts—and more.

Let me tell you—that one little moment is worth the rest of a lifetime! Give in to it! For what if it happens to be the truth— that following Jesus, dying the death, is all there is to life, that the rest is bogus, cheap and tawdry? Then you'd best follow, hadn't you? Then you'd be a fool to let the power and the glory slip for the kind of pottage that contents most men. "Follow me," he says, "follow me!" Get out of your boat and on your feet. Discipleship is what you were made for, discipleship is what you're summoned to, discipleship is what that curious thing called theology's all about—plain vanilla, garden variety, beautiful discipleship of Jesus—nothing more. Rise up and follow, and it'll be the first creation all over again!

Coda

And he said to them, "Do not be amazed; you seek Jesus of Nazareth, who was crucified. He has risen, he is not here; see the place where they laid him. (Mark 16:6)

The first dealer in words, the first lexicographer you or I had anything to do with, describes the coda in a musical piece as a "concluding passage." Now that's an anemic, bloodless way to put it—it's like defining Abraham Lincoln as a bony, bearded bi-ped. We've got to fill out the definition a bit, because the coda, the "concluding passage" is where we're at right now, and putting the finish to something we began four years ago requires more than Noah Webster would concede. In a coda, the old, basic theme, struck near the beginning of the piece, perhaps varied, embellished throughout it, is taken up once more in a last, final burst of sound.

What was our theme? Worship in Israel, exegetical method, Wittenberg and Rome, the church and war, homiletics, counseling or ministry to minorities? None of these—these all served the theme, were subordinate to it. Theology was not meant to be done for its own sake—the music of McNamara's band would have been something less than grand if the only notes written were for McCarthy's old bassoon. A statement in an official church paper once read that however a man might interpret the words, the fact remains we are saved by our stewardship. Substitute for that worthy project any one of a thousand other causes, concerns and programs, and the scene is the same—some McCarthy, pumping out a series of belches in the base clef and pretending for all the world as though God had anointed him soloist.

. The theme is the gospel, the evangel—this is the thesis, the text, the topic by which all those other things, those other strains are meant to be ruled. And since there's no guarantee you or I will ever come together for another coda, it's time to play loud—if not well!—and to choose some part of that grand theme requires every bit of wind and energy we've got. So, let's get our stands in place, dog-ear the pages, pick up our instruments, and, to mix the metaphor, get ready to pitch headlong into the good news!

"He has risen!" Drums, horns, cymbals and tympani! But risen where? Where else but into space and time? The resurrection of Jesus of Nazareth is not an other-worldly thing. We are not the devotees of a religion who celebrate the rising of their god as a feat accomplished by him in some private, celestial sphere of his own and bully for him, something we can only re-enact or pantomime, in which we participate by exalting ourselves to where he is—"Do not say in your heart, 'Who will ascend into heaven?' that is, to bring Christ down." The fact that we cannot establish the resurrection by historical-critical means, that we can merely indicate the probabilities, that as historians we can only say some believed they saw him alive, does not make the resurrection an other-worldly thing, outside our life and pain. Let it be incredible, unbelievable, unimaginable, but let it be so in our own space and time. Let it sum up and crown every other incredible thing which has happened to us, and whose explanation strains consent and belief, but let it be there where Matthew, Mark, Luke

and John set it—in midst of bread and fish and cakes and camp-
fires and frightened women, rumors and unbelief and soldiers
bribed to deny it—in the corporeal, the earthly, the profane,
vulnerable to the critic's scrutiny, but there, where we are!

Nor is Jesus' resurrection some happy ending that makes for
cozy reading of his life and death. I love detective novels, but
can't restrain that urge to thumb to the last page to see whether
or not Hercule Poirot or Miss Marple or Lord Peter Wimsey
has come through it all in one piece. My comfort demands it.
And to see Paul Newman blown to bits in the final scene of
"Butch Cassidy" offends against that rule. But it is not that way
with the resurrection! Those of you with palates educated dif-
ferently than mine will understand. That event is not the happy
ending somehow vindicates his life or answers the question of
his cross. It is not the thing to make sense of his proclamation of
the kingdom come, of his love, his eating with tax collectors and
sinners, his call to follow, his teaching or miracles—it is the other
way around! It is his death that makes sense of his rising! Who
heard the word "He is not here"? Those who came to anoint his
corpse! Who saw him! Those who had penetrated to his secret
at the ministry and death! Why did he rise with wounds—"put
your finger here," he said, "and see my hands; and put out your
hand, and place it in my side"—the *cross* was his exaltation! Before the agony he prayed, "Father, the hour has come; glorify
thy Son"; when he hung his head and died, the earth shook,
rocks were split and tombs opened—the resurrection is the apoc-
alypse of his cross! He did not die so that he could rise! He rose
because he died! He was "obedient unto death . . . therefore God
highly exalted him"! And this means that entropy or whatever
in the world it is we all suffer, tears and wearing away and death,
is at the heart of *God's* own life! God raised Jesus from the dead,
raised him into our earth and time, and, not in some second,

extra thing but in a "Yes!" and an "Amen!" to his taking on our flesh and pain. A chorus or two of horns here, and more drums!

Now if Jesus' rising is the clue to death as the way of God's own life, and not just the last truth of our existence, then, for all of me, to say "Jesus died" is the same as to say "Jesus is Lord," then when that word of the cross is heard God is marked as sovereign and supreme, for wherever that word is, the origin, the beginning, the core and essence of life itself is exposed! Then, wherever that word is trusted and that smashing, ruining and destroying through which the whole universe is being created and made new is affirmed in one little life, the ring is closed and nothing but God, God's name, God's kingdom, God's will remains! Then "I am crucified with Christ," and "it is no longer I who live, but Christ in me!" Then there is only that word to be lisped, told, dramatized, piped, sung, whistled, danced to and believed!

And by that rising his death touches all. It includes even the worst, embraces men with no virtue at all to lose, no goodness to betray, no piety, no religion to abandon, men with no treason left to commit. But then God is the God of the godless—a truth of our faith not often conceded or confessed, but the juiciest part of it for all that and good news, brothers, good news! "While we were enemies we were reconciled to God by the death of his Son!"

There's a new piety abroad, and in formal structure, at least, it is identical to the old. Both types seek their criterion for truth in the innards, in "feeling" as such, in the "gut-level." Both lay down conditions for membership—the one that a man point to the date of his conversion, the other that he be under thirty. Both demand empirical proof of conversion in things done or undone. But if we can't feel, can't point to this or that, are over thirty (more's the pity!) and can adduce proof of nothing, what then? Are we only grey lumps for all the braying asses in the world to kick? We can be sinners! And that, as Luther once said, is something a man isn't by nature—from any human point of view, that is. Christ died and Christ rose and God is the God of those, principally, above all—now that's a ludicrous way to put it; how can he be more of God for one than the other? Well, let it be ludicrously put, there's ample biblical evidence for this kind of tomfoolery—above all the God of those who acknowledge their total poverty before him and before every other man! Jesus said: "Blessed are the poor in spirit, for theirs is the kingdom of heaven"—"You who affirm your poverty from the heart, to you, I who stand like Moses at the gate of the heavenly land will give the kingdom, the future world!" He rose, so his death is all and touches all, and the godless, the godless above all! Rattle the drums and play the flute and pump the bass and blare away!

During the very last of his study for the ministry in New Haven, the nineteen year old Jonathan Edwards penned some resolutions, the sixth of which reads: "Resolved, To live with all my might, while I do live." That resolution is grouped with others which arise from a historical context vastly different than our own and in ways reflect an understanding of faith far below that of his maturer years. Still, what grips me about the setting from which I've lifted this little gem, is its intent, its pledge that the life of Jonathan Edwards shall be a kind of death. "Resolved, To enquire every night, before I go to bed, whether I have acted in the best way I possibly could, with respect to eating and drinking." That's a kind of death. "Never to suffer the least motions of anger toward irrational beings." That too. "In narrations, never speak anything but the pure and simple verity." That too, at least for me! "Let there be something of benevolence, in all that I speak." Death again. "To improve every opportunity, when I am in the best and happiest frame of mind,

to cast and venture my soul on the Lord Jesus Christ. . . ."
Again! "Resolved, That I will act so, in every respect as I think
I shall wish I had done, if I should at last be damned." Some day
read that beautiful biography of Edwards by Perry Miller and
see if the whole life of that great heart was not a dying!

He rose, so his death is his coronation; he rose, so the word
of his cross spells the essence of things; he rose, so he died for all,
for the godless, and now, there's nothing left but for you to close
the ring, to affirm the truth of his rising in your own death. My
good fellow! I hope, when the justice you seek now has become
your children's tyrant, when finally no other human being can
give what you need or needs what you give, when what you
have planned has turned to ashes, when you are finally convinced
that what you have done will never in all the world be remembered, when tomorrow means anonymity and failure—I hope that
then there will be nothing left of you but an ache and burning
for God in every sinew and nerve, for then you'll have begun to
die; then his resurrection will have begun to be announced in
you, then you'll be fit for life and for love! "He has risen!"
Christ has risen! Hallelujah! There's the coda! Now let it ring
a little while in the rafters!

Death in My Future

> Now it happened that as he was praying alone the disciples were with him; and he asked them, "Who do the people say that I am?" And they answered, "John the Baptist; but others say, Elijah; and others, that one of the old prophets has risen." And he said to them, "But who do you say that I am?" And Peter answered, "The Christ of God." But he charged and commanded them to tell this to no one, saying, "The Son of man must suffer many things, and be rejected by the elders and chief priests and scribes, and be killed, and on the third day be raised." And he said to all, "If any man would come after me, let him deny himself and take up his cross daily and follow me. For whoever would save his life will lose it; and whoever loses his life for my sake, he will save it. (Luke 9:18-24).

This brief passage in Luke is simple enough to grasp. Confess Christ, confess him doomed to die, and await the same fate for yourself. Three points—one, two, three—and needing only a bit of gingerbread to claim your attention at the first, and something to round it off at the last.

If I have a theology, and that's been doubted a time or two, it finds exposition in these three little points. But "having" a theology in terms of adopting a view is one thing, and allowing it to rattle up from the marrow of my bones is quite another. I *consent* to these words of Christ; sometimes even take delight in them—they make it possible for me to look at God, myself and a host of other things in some kind of meaningful perspective. I would even venture the notion that anyone who cannot root his

42

reflection about God, the world and others in such words will himself perhaps be saved, but only as through fire!

But I find "in my members," as another ancient has it, "another law at war with the law of my mind." After a day of hammering away at what's popularly dubbed the "theology of the cross," I lie awake at night, torn by doubt, fearful of death to the point of requiring medical assistance, anxious lest, as happened with one old schoolmate and colleague, I may have "shot my wad," and it's then I turn to hate these words of Christ. *I will not die*—to myself, my dreams, those few precious notions it's taken me more years than I'd care to count to hatch, die to wants, to needing recognition, if not in your eyes then in someone else's. Lean back and let it happen, allow the Almighty to beat the living bejabbers out of me—what is that but pronouncing some wretched benediction on the status quo? If blacks and Chicanos and libbers and little old ladies in tennis shoes and homosexuals and Standard Oil can identify the cause of men and whatever gods may be with their own, demand integration, identity, integrity and independence, then why in God's name not I?

The reason, I suspect, is that he'll not let me go! I've denied him, disobeyed him, turned my back on him, even blasphemed, I think, but he won't let go. Give the condition whatever horizontal interpretation you choose—abnormal function of the glands, psychosis (masochism might do for a starter)—I'm still on his leash. That's why the meaning of that "if" in the clause "if any man would come after me," or the meaning of that "whoever" in the clause next—"whoever loses his life for my sake"—still escapes me. For when did I ever have a choice? He made his mark on me even before my navel had healed! And since he won't let go, death is in my future, one way or another. The trouble with that old Dutch doctrine of the eternal perseverance of the saints is that it assumed the saints, not God would persevere.

But what if all this dying is for something? Not merely for the hope old Abe expressed long ago at Gettysburg, "that these dead shall not have died in vain"—great heaven! he was a tortured, dying thing himself, wasn't he? What if all this being grasped, throttled and squeezed, and all the cries and doubts and terror attendant upon it should somehow culminate in one grand resurrection! In volume two of his dual work, Luke has Peter say: "Brethren, Christ was not abandoned to Hades, nor did his flesh see corruption. God raised him up, made him both Lord and Christ, this Jesus whom you crucified!" What if the same should occur with me, with you? Then, in the grip, in the jaws of God would be the place to be, then doubt would be the thing to endure, then the night without light as good a time as in the sun, then dragging the cross better than lounging on the throne —remember how Napoleon crowned himself emperor of all the French at Notre Dame?—then the loss of the whole world better than the forfeit of self! Elsewhere in Luke Peter announced, "Lord, I am ready to go with you to prison and to death." He didn't mean it then, but one day his friends found him impaled and upside down, in macabre imitation of his Lord.

One of the best once said that when Jesus calls a man he bids him come and die. I'll die then, and so will you, held fast in that awful hand, but waiting for the glory, waiting for the kingdom, power and glory!

There'll Be Some Changes Made

There was a rich man, who was clothed in purple and fine linen and who feasted sumptuously every day. And at his gate lay a poor man named Lazarus, full of sores, who desired to be fed with what fell from the rich man's table; moreover the dogs came and licked his sores. The poor man died and was carried by the angels to Abraham's bosom. The rich man also died and was buried; and in Hades, being in torment, he lifted up his eyes, and saw Abraham far off and Lazarus in his bosom. And he called out, 'Father Abraham, have mercy upon me, and send Lazarus to dip the end of his finger in water and cool my tongue; for I am in anguish in this flame.' But Abraham said, 'Son, remember that you in your lifetime received your good things, and Lazarus in like manner evil things; but now he is comforted here, and you are in anguish. And besides all this, between us and you a great chasm has been fixed, in order that those who would pass from here to you may not be able, and none may cross from there to us.' And he said, 'Then I beg you, father, to send him to my father's house, for I have five brothers, so that he may warn them, lest they also come into this place of torment.' But Abraham said, 'They have Moses and the prophets; let them hear them.' And he said, 'No, father Abraham; but if some one goes to them from the dead, they will repent.' He said to him, 'If they do not hear Moses and the prophets, neither will they be convinced if some one should rise from the dead. (Luke 16:19-31)

The first chapter of Genesis says that after God had made everything, he looked around and saw that it was "very good."

45

That doesn't mean every polliwog was already a frog or every deer already had its antlers. It doesn't mean there'd be no growth in that world God made. It means simply that everything he made would turn out as he'd planned.

The world isn't that way any longer. Any resemblance between our planet and that world God made is sheer accident. I'm not going to trouble your heads with tallying up the things that make our world so monstrously different from what God had in mind. You've got eyes in your head; you can see the museum of horrors this place has become, and you ought to have an ache in your soul at the wrong and pain and blood and death dogging all of life.

But what you can't see, perhaps, or what you don't feel is that *God* is discontented with the world as it is, that *God's* in a state over the way things have turned out, and that he's been in that anguish almost since life began. Early on, things had come to such a pass he "was sorry that he had made man on the earth, and it grieved him to his heart." *God's* in a torment that there should be Lazaruses in the world—men full of sores who hanker after crumbs, while rich men dress in purple and fine linen and fill their bellies to bursting.

It won't help to try and figure out how or why things got this way, won't help to blame the devil or the Russians or the Republican party, because, as certain as death and taxes, someone's going to come along and ask, "who let the devil or the Russians or the Republicans into Paradise in the first place; if God is so almighty powerful, why didn't he take steps to prevent evil's ever entering our world?" And you'd be left with your finger in your mouth and your head swimming. The question of the why and how of evil is a deep, dark riddle, and there's not a man alive or dead who has ever solved it. One thing is clear—if you could see the tragic train of events your own little life has set in motion, it'd throw you in a dark despair! But it's too late for recriminations. We got nowhere running about with the Queen of Hearts, accusing all and sundry and yelling "off with their heads, off with their heads!" It's enough to know God's in an anguish over the way things are.

There's something else you'd best know about God. He has an affinity for men like the Lazarus of our parable. He is attracted to the hungry and naked and suffering and captive and dying. Now, that's a strange God, whose heart beats for the imperfect, the twisted and the malformed! Every other god you hear or read about is in a hot sweat for beauty and perfection and isosceles triangles and thirty-two inch waists. Not this God, not the God of Luke's Gospel. He has an affinity for Lazarus.

And so, he's making changes! You heard what happened to Lazarus. He ended up in "Abraham's bosom," so the ancient story reads. That scabby, scrofulous, crumb-picking nobody ended up getting "comforted," while the rich man found himself in Tartarus. What an amazing reversal of conditions! The man who had nothing suddenly woke with everything, and the man who had everything suddenly woke with worse than nothing. Let it be a lesson—the "righteous" man, the "noble" and "decent" man you'd think could stand erect before the Almighty and demand a promotion to heavenly bliss finds himself in torment, while the "sinner" passes nice as you please through those pearly gates.

Long before her baby was born, poor little Mary sang a hymn to those amazing changes God would make: "He has scattered the proud in the imagination of their hearts," she sang, "he has put down the mighty from their thrones, and exalted those of low degree; he has filled the hungry with good things, and the rich he has sent empty away!" Every page of Luke's Gospel, almost, to say nothing of all of Holy Writ, is a celebration of that reversal of conditions which obtains with God. It's plumb full of stories of folks with invitations to dinner who never get to eat, and folks without them who feast like kings. Friends, brothers and kinsmen are omitted from the guest-list, while the poor, the maimed, the lame and the blind take first seats. Israel, with its law and prophets is denied the mighty Rule of God, while barbarians and slaves throng into it. Sinners, not righteous are called to repentance, and the stone rejected by the builders becomes the head of the corner—everything is turned upside down, topsy-turvy, this way and that with this God!

Do you know where these changes are being made? Do you know who or what the lever is God is using to get this world off dead center? Do you know the measure he's using, the scale, the balance by which he makes the old new and the new old; by which he fills valleys, brings low mountains and hills, straightens the crooked and smooths out rough places—stands the whole world on its head? *Another Lazarus*—he who was rich, but for our sakes became poor! And it wasn't only purple, fine linen and dainties he left behind—it was godhead, omniscience, power, unbelievable power he let go! And it wasn't merely that he came, angel-like, simply to *announce* that Someone up there in the sky doesn't reckon by any human standards but loves what men hate—peace and mercy and a humble heart, and hates what men love—pomp and pride and the will to rule. He himself suffered that reversal of conditions in his own life, his own self! And, what's more, he revelled in it! It became him, it was second-nature to him, it squared with what he is, with the stuff of which he's made. Jesus, a Lazarus from nowhere in particular, born to no one in particular, living and dying at no time in particular—he's the One in whom the Almighty's making changes! He's the scale, the measure, the balance—he's God's lever to get the world, the universe, off dead center.

Christ became a Lazarus to make us rich; contracted sores, ate crumbs and lived with dogs so we might wear the royal purple and live like kings! Now that's a bit of news a man could spend time mulling over, could let soak in the juices of his head; that's a bit of news to revel in, sing and shout and dance about, but the truth our parable means to hammer home is wherever the consciousness of that "happy exchange" between Christ and us has dawned on a man and gripped him to the marrow of his bones, that man's off like a streak to exchange his role with another. For it follows as night the day—where there's trust in Christ, love for Christ, there's love for the other as well. If in Christ you're free and sovereign, a most free lord of all, clad in purple, in him you're also bound to the other, you're the other's slave. If, by the mighty power of his Spirit, you've traveled past yourself to God, past your rights, past your goodness, past your religion and your piety—if you've left all that baggage behind and in Jesus Christ have taken hold of God and him alone, then you're off to travel past yourself again, this time to the other and him alone! To be in Christ, to follow him, press his case, plead his cause, means to be for the other and to the self totally indifferent.

Turn that coin around. If there's no exchange of roles with another, no love for another, no being bound to the other, no travelling past oneself to him, then there's no faith, no trust, no love, no freedom, no having travelled past oneself to God, no life in God. And, nothing else will do the trick—not even miracles! "I've five brothers back there," howled the rich man, "send Lazarus back from his grave to scare them into voting Medicare, food stamps and government housing, or they'll all go to hell for sure!" And Abraham said, "if they don't hear Moses and the prophets, they won't be convinced if someone pops out of his grave."

But will our love change the world, the whole world? Will it make a difference? How often haven't we heard that question from all the tight-fisted, penny-pinching crabs of the world? But the question is presumptuous, just plain presumptuous, for it's *God* who's making the changes. It's *his* name that's being hallowed, *his* kingdom that's coming, *his* will that's being done, his power, his glory, his love reflected in the face of Christ which furnishes the fulcrum and lever to move the earth.

Never mind about your love's making a difference to the *world*—it'll make all the difference in the world to *you!* Your destiny hangs on it! I suppose a nation must proceed according to its own "enlightened self-interest." I suppose a nation can't afford to drown its enemies in butter and eggs, ham and cheese rather than in bullets and bombs, though you've got to admit it'd be unique; crazy, perhaps, but unique and no crazier than the way in which nations have behaved till now. But leaving such happy prospects to the dreamers, to your children, perhaps, it is enough now for you to mark that *your* fate, *your* future hangs on your loving the other! No time after you've breathed your last to remedy the lack. No way then to close the gap between what you are and what you might be—a lover. No chance then at another hand of cards. Old Abe hollered over into that blazing hell, "between us and you there's a gulf, a chasm and those who want to get from us to you can't, and none can get from you to us."

While you're still breathing, still puffing in and out, you've a chance to share in a new creating. For God's doing a great and mighty thing—he's making changes, altering the face of the earth. Not so you can see it, but as sure as he made heaven and earth it's happening. The thing's hidden, hidden deeply enough to make some wonder if it's really there, to make some disbelieve and trade it for some half-baked, starry-eyed, man-made scheme, but it's there, it's happening. In Jesus Christ, become Lazarus for us, God's after standing the earth on its head, he's after kneading and pounding and shaping it like fresh dough into what he intended it to be. And, you can share the new and fresh and green; you can become a co-creator, you can get a piece of the action'll transform welts and sores to purple, crumbs to feasts, grief to glory, death to life, the kingdom of this world to the kingdom of God! Give heart and life to Christ, and love to your neighbor.

Remembrance

(For a Communion at my Father's former Parish)

And when the hour came, he sat at table, and the apostles with him. And he said to them, "I have earnestly desired to eat this passover with you before I suffer; for I tell you I shall not eat it until it is fulfilled in the kingdom of God." And he took a cup, and when he had given thinks he said, "Take this, and divide it among yourselves; for I tell you that from now on I shall not drink of the fruit of the vine until the kingdom of God comes." And he took bread, and when he had given thanks he broke it and gave it to them, saying, "This is my body. But behold the hand of him who betrays me is with me on the table." (Luke 22:14-21)

Man is a rememberer. And so are ants and dogs and cats and fish and elephants. But only man is able to give his memory extension—in the computer, in the remembering machine. And there are as many ways to remember things as there are things to remember. The ancient Jew used the mnemonic device. He chose the first letter of the first word of each phrase to be remembered and built the whole into nonsense syllables. "Vibgyor" —that's a mnemonic device. It means absolutely nothing, but it does represent all the colors of the rainbow: violet, indigo, blue, green, yellow, orange and red. And how many of you have not twitted your wives with their outrageous remembrance by association: "Oh yes! Alice's birthday is on the twenty-second; that's the day the streetcars stopped running in Minneapolis; Gertrude and I got holes in our stockings dashing for the last car from Bryant to Lake, and when I got home Fred had his gallbladder attack." There are many ways to remember.

I want to tell you about three of those ways. First, there's the remembrance of nostalgia. In the last act of Shakespeare's *Hamlet,* the gloomy prince, after brief exile in England, appears in a churchyard where some clowns are digging a grave, spies a skull he recognizes, picks it up and says: "Alas, poor Yorick!" There's nostalgia in his remembering: "Here hung those lips that I have kissed I know not how oft. Where be your gibes now? your gambols? your songs? your flashes of merriment, that were wont to set the tables on a roar?"

You and I indulge in that kind of remembering. When I remember my father, how he looked, what he said and did, I sometimes give way to nostalgia. Sometimes, I rummage about in the stuff he left behind, his old Bibles, say, and have myself a wistful moment, a moment of hankering for some lost, long-ago moment when he was in the flesh; a hankering for the funny times, the silly, roaring, belly-laugh times mothers and wives don't always see and if they do don't always want to remember, and the great times, the something-stuck-in-your-throat times.

I succumb to nostalgia. But so does the church! That little hymn we used to sing—"I think, when I read that sweet story of old, when Jesus was here among men, How he called little children as lambs to his fold, I should like to have been with them then," and stanza two: "I wish that his hands had been placed on my head, That his arm had been thrown a-round me. . . ."—that, bless your heart, is nostalgia with a vengeance! And the presupposition? The underlying, ruling notion behind it all? It's the idea that the past, the days dead and gone, were the best. In the church, the days of Jesus' flesh were the "good old days" for some; for others they were the age of the apostles; for others again the first "Christian" century; for still others the time of Luther—ah, them were the days!—and for others still, fifty years ago when no one talked of the death of God or the new morality or racial injustice or care of the earth or the immorality of war. Each age, each generation of the church has had its nostalgic, hankering crew for which the past was best of all.

There's another kind of remembering, twin-sister to the first, yet dissimilar. It's not a remembering that has to do with just harking back or fondling souvenirs. There's a busy-ness about it. It's a remembering that involves reliving in some kinetic fashion what happened yesterday. You might call it the remembrance of recital. You and I remember in this fashion too. My father was great for epigrams. Some days I rather considered him a sort of Johnny Appleseed, strewing the earth, not with apple seeds, but with epigrams. I'd return home with a respectable report card, and against the background of what was a normally "checkered" academic career would begin to crow, only to hear that "the sun at midday casts no shadow." Or, "you'll be a man before your mother." Or, I'd complain about the weather and be told to "talk to God about it." Epigrams! Yet the older I become, the more I find myself dealing in the same coin, as though my own life were in some way a recital of his.

And the church recites! A good bit of religion, any kind of religion, traffics in recital. Good Friday among Christians is an example. That one day in the year witnesses the most massive recitation in all the western world. Everybody, or almost, pretends as though that were the very day on which Jesus was crucified. Even preachers get themselves up like Peter and Pontius Pilate, give Peter and Pontius Pilate soliloquies on successive Wednesdays and get their pictures in the *Lutheran Standard*. Every *Sunday* is a recital, not only of that first Easter, but of each day of our lives. The daily guilt, the consciousness of it, the cry for help, the release and the resultant joy—these are all recited, re-enacted in that queer, formal and archaic language we call our liturgy. Every Communion at which we huddle together in rows waiting for the body and blood—that's a recital. Did not Jesus say: "Do this in remembrance of me"? And the presupposition? The underlying, ruling notion behind it all might be that the present is nothing but a repetition of the past, is only the past's turning back upon itself like the point of a pencil in a drawn circle, the sort of notion that's even defended in Ecclesiastes: "What has been is what will be, and what has been done is what will be done; and there is nothing new under the sun." If with the first kind of remembering the past is always best, with this second kind, twin sister to the first, history is always repeating itself.

Now I can think of nothing more abhorrent, more destructive of life than if you or I should remember in only these two ways. We would turn the whole earth into a museum and sentence ourselves to hopelessness, men caught and trapped by what is old, or damned merely to its repetition! When I lived in Iowa, lobotomies were the rage. If a man or woman was in psychic chaos, it was assumed the only thing for it was to rip the connections in his frontal lobes with a tool which looked for all the world like an awl. The immediate crisis was met, but the lobotomy left him incapable of projecting himself into the future. Nostalgic remembering or remembering by recital is all such folk have left to do.

There's another kind of remembering, the kind hurls a man forward, makes him strain toward some future thing, makes him dream and give legs to his dream. It's the remembrance of some promise, some vision not yet come into its own, dangling out there in front of him, like a check, still waiting to be cashed. That's a remembering that fills a man with expectancy, impatience, breathlessness, may even make him violent! Those old lines of Emma Lazarus on the Statue of Liberty— "Give me your tired, your poor, Your huddled masses yearning to breathe free. . . . I lift my lamp beside the golden door"—a man would have to be blind as a bat not to see that for some (whatever it is those words reflect—reception, warmth, freedom, opportunity) they are a promise still unfulfilled, a vision still unrealized, but a promise still able to fire a man with taste enough for its fulfillment that he'll shed blood for it! The longer we persist in requiring further identification from men who would "cash in" on such promises, the longer we enact legislation calculated to delay that vision's realization, the longer we retain in office men committed to that dream's delay, the sooner we will destroy all dreaming, all promise, and ourselves with it.

Now you and I here, we remember in this third fashion too. We remember words which throw us into the tomorrows. Yesterday you were promised tomorrow's sale, last month you were promised next month's raise, last year you were promised next year's three weeks' off, ten years ago you were promised retirement with comfort or the head cashier's post in the decade next. Think! Let it soak a while in the juices of your mind! You live by remembering promises! According to gerontologists hereabouts, old men die principally because they've too long a wait between birthdays—they rot to the socket because they cannot retain a word spoken yesterday about what will happen tomorrow.

And the church, the community of Christ remembers in this way, in this way above all! Jesus said: "I shall not eat it until it is fulfilled in the kingdom of God . . . I shall not drink of the fruit of the vine until the kingdom of God comes." The kingdom had come, right enough, it had come with Jesus of Naza-

reth—still and all, it had not yet come! And if Jesus did not eat
or drink with his little company on the eve of his death, that
would only give signal illustration to the fact that for him there
was something more to come, some manifestation of God not
yet seen or heard. And how he strained toward it! That which
his Father was still to do in future carried him crying "My God,
my God" right through the pain and the black darkness. The
God who appeared to Moses in the burning bush and said "I
will be who I will be," an Exodus God, a bedouin, roving God,
not a paunchy, sedentary God like the gods of the Canaanites or
like Buddha, but a lean and jealous God of the tomorrows who
catapulted the Hebrew children into possession of the land with
promises and commanded them to their realization, that same
God promised his Son Jesus a kingdom, power and glory for the
sake of which he "endured the cross, despising the shame." But
that kingdom, power and glory are still not yet his! The fulfillment is still in the offing, still imminent, still the matter of the
next moment, day or hour. Jesus is not yet what he will be; God
is not yet what he will be. The remembrance of the word which
promises—"I shall not eat until it is fulfilled"—that word which
gives the only sense to what we do, that kind of remembrance,
is what keeps the community of Christ alive. Not just alive to
yearn for the future! When Jesus healed the deaf, the dumb, the
blind, the lame and raised the dead, he was *anticipating* the future! So that kind of remembrance keeps us alive to give some
fulfillment to that word in the present, like Jesus, to wrench
away some piece of the future and plant it in the "here and now,"
to give the hungry food, the thirsty drink, to welcome the
stranger, clothe the naked, visit the sick, free the captive, and
not just keep oneself "unstained from the world"—by vote or
prayer, legislation, or meditation to approximate that day when

he will be what he will be: "King of Kings and Lord of Lords," God, "everything in everyone"! And then wait for that word, that promise, to which you give the very most in you, and hosts of others like you. That's what's to be remembered!

Between the Tree and the Bark

(Communion)

And he took bread, and when he had given thanks he broke it and gave it to them, saying, "This is my body." (Luke 22:19).

I'd rather not have God in the world, if you don't mind my saying so. A God should be beyond or beneath or behind the world, though our capsules and whatchamacallits make even that possibility more and more remote. At any rate, a God ought to be somewhere out in the blue, past the quasars, riding over earths and heavens like ancient Thor, with thunderbolts in his hand. And what's here on earth, well, that ought simply to furnish some kind of analogy to that lofty Deity, some memory of him perhaps evoked by the face of a beautiful woman, a sight of the stars, a Beethoven sonata or a baby brought to the birth. But not in the world, in bread and wine and water, in the life and story of a martyred man. Because if he's here, then he's got no place to stand from which to get any kind of purchase on the world. Everyone knows that if he wants to move some great, huge thing, he needs a fulcrum and somewhere to stand beyond it. And, too, if God is here, what's to protect him against the wear and tear, against obsolescence and a thousand crucifixions? I'd rather not have God in the world. Let him

59

talk to me as folks suppose he talks to David Wilkerson—from "away beyond the blue"—but not in the simple narrative of an Amos or Hosea, stories critics can fuss and fumble with. Or, let those stories at least fall straight from heaven, like the Koran, writ with the finger of Allah, blessed be He, clean quit of this-worldliness, as one pseudo-Lutheran statement of recent origin suggests. And as for this meagre "meal" we're about to share, let it be as Zwingli and all his tribe have said it is—a symbol or sign of some other, truly "heavenly" reality.

But all the while I'd rather not have him here—vulnerable, helpless as a child in its crib and braying asses all 'round, I've a hunger for him which is like a fire can't be put out, and I'm not different from you or any other man or woman. So I'm between the tree and the bark, or as the old King James has it, I'm in a "strait betwixt the two,"—not at all warm to the notion of God's presence in the world, and yet desperately in need of him.

Now, the more I think of it, between the two is perhaps where I belong. For one thing's sure, if God had remained high and lifted up, as in the prophet's vision, I could never have risen to him. The second stanza of an old Latin hymn begins: "Given from on high to me, I cannot rise to thee." If he'd not come down, I could never have found him there on heavenly ground. I can't even find *my own* way here on earth! So, while I do not want him here, yet could never ascend to him if he were not, he makes his appearance in the rude objects of my everyday existence—in the water, bread and wine. He gives himself to me in such pedestrian fashion because he knows I'm without a ladder or a tower. Down he comes, in such mean, crude things— because he loves me. Now, that's a poor and miserable way for a God to behave! But I must trade my perplexity and embarrass-ment at his puny epiphany for the recognition that he knows me and cares what happens to my frail and feeble flesh. Could *this* be the fulcrum, the lever to raise the earth—his love?

The Good Book says there'll come a time when that betwixt and between will be a memory, when this lowly, suffering God will be what has never entered heart or mind—will be beyond or beneath or behind all that is, enthroned on an Olympus higher than ever Homer dreamed for his Zeus, robed in a great and splendid light, when the pain of his descent will have been exchanged for a thousand joys! And before that infinite God we'll cast our crowns one by one beside the glassy sea and shout: "To him who sits upon the throne and to the Lamb be blessing and honor and glory and might for ever and ever!" And not because we imagined it, dreamed it, willed it, but because of his love. But for now, betwist and between is where we belong.

There's a Father for You!

And he came out, and went, as was his custom, to the Mount of Olives; and the disciples followed him. And when he came to the place he said to them, "Pray that you may not enter into temptation." And he withdrew from them about a stone's throw, and knelt down and prayed, "Father, if thou art willing, remove this cup from me; nevertheless, not my will, but thine, be done." And there appeared to him an angel from heaven, strengthening him. And being in an agony he prayed more earnestly; and his sweat became like great drops of blood falling down upon the ground. And when he rose from prayer, he came to the disciples and found them sleeping for sorrow, and he said to them, "Why do you sleep? Rise and pray that you may not enter into temptation." (Luke 22:39-46)

There's not much to Luke's record of Jesus' last night alive. It's the briefest in all the Gospels. Luke wasn't much for dawdling or hanging about the Mount of Olives, like some Holy Land tourist gone to get his money's worth with snapshots of Uncle Charlie and Auntie Kate by some gnarled, half-rotten tree that marks the spot where Jesus prayed. He wasn't much for that sort of thing—more for getting the thing down without the gingerbread and moving on. But if Luke was in a hurry with his story, he didn't omit the harsh detail. When you match his narrative with that of Mark or Matthew, it takes first prize for grimness.

Long ago, this story in Luke struck some in the church as a mite too grim, so they omitted the verses dealing with the helping angel and the sweat like drops of blood. Like television censors who edit sex and horror films so as not to offend the sensitive viewer, those "ancient authorities" expunged from the record the gloomier aspects of the scene. And, after all, "God loves winners!" and Jesus was a winner, wasn't he? He didn't need celestial assistance, and his fright and doubt didn't ooze from every pore. He knew God would pull a rabbit out of the hat in the end. Well, those ancient fellows who leave out verses 43 and 44 won't have their way. The grimness belongs there; it's stuck fast in the tradition.

When you sweep away all the holy smoke which centuries of treating the Scripture like a centerpiece have made to swirl around it, when you drive back behind all the immortal prose of its innumerable translators and get down to the bare bones, what's here is a portrait of Jesus who tears himself free of his friends in a torrent of feeling and passion, kneeling like a beggar, bargaining with God for his life, and bleeding an agony of doubt and fear. The picture isn't something that could be reckoned to the advantage of an ordinary man. Indeed, such stuff is what the loss of vice-presidential nominations is made of! Big boys don't cry; men aren't afraid!

But what of Jesus, in the words of one famous gentleman, "the only incomparably great man powerful enough to conceive himself spiritual leader of mankind and seize history?" Such a scene as this made Albert Schweitzer sick to the marrow and take off for Lambarene in search for some alternative to this praying, haggling Messiah. And long before that genius was ever a kiss on his grandmother's cheek, that parcel of folks that calls itself Christian had to wrestle with an audience that wouldn't abide the story of a bleeding Jesus. The passion's always been the thing to stick in the craw. Not even Christians can suppress the urge to tell the happy ending, to idealize the death out of all proportion, to mitigate the blood and sweat. You and I may care no more for this scene than did Schweitzer.

What was that agony, doubt and terror all about? If I'd been Jesus, it would have been fear for my own precious, little life! Now, don't tell me I've no need to be afraid, or recommend the reading of Elizabeth Kübler-Ross who describes the stages of anguish, of let's pretend and of submission every man or woman with a terminal disease goes through. My doctor says I'm nowhere near dying, I'm still full of fuss and feathers, just like Jesus there, and I've a mountain-sized aversion to the notion of my being lowered into the ground while a few sad-faced friends go off to their coffee and cookies. Indeed, God will be there, he'll be there, standing behind the veil, and I've moments when that thought gives unbelievable comfort, but I'm a human being with an appetite to persist, to live, to puff in and out. But I'm not Jesus, you can thank your lucky stars, and it's useless to attempt plumbing the depths of his consciousness on the basis of my own pitiful self-understanding.

Still and all, Luke gives us a clue to what was in his mind when he writes that Jesus twice called his friends to prayer. If in that hideous night he could forget himself and his agony long enough to care for them, then that agony might have had nothing to do with himself. Then that fear might have had nothing in it of my own. What if the doubt sprang from the apprehension that with his death the Almighty'd foreclose on his people's mortgage? All through this Gospel, Jesus is up to his blessed eyes calling the self-righteous and stiff-necked to mark the distance between themselves and God, to let him have his throne, to walk into his kingdom through the gate marked "lost sheep, lost coin and prodigal."

What if Jerusalem, killer of prophets and builder of their tombs was headed for doom, and the weight of it broke his mighty heart? And what if the few who seemed to hear and understand were totally unprepared to have his cause handed them? What if his sense of their appalling exposure to all those powers which assaulted and came near crushing him, drove him to a frenzy of questioning? It wouldn't be long when they'd be alone, unprotected, needing wallet and purse, facing want and conflict, needing a sword! And it'd be no glorious battle they'd be heading for, with a "once more unto the breach dear friends, once more; Or close the wall up with our English dead!" and trumpets and victory and "Harry, England and St. George" at the end of it. What if the agony had to do with them, with *us,* "frail children of dust and feeble as frail?" That would have been like him—to be in an awful doubt and fear for someone else. By framing Jesus' agony with that twice-repeated call to prayer, Luke has given us the clue that that passion was not just for himself. At the beginning and end there's that word: "Pray that you may not enter into temptation."

But if it's no mere private grief we're peeking in on here, if the agony's for someone else, then that prayer which gets the lion's share in this little piece is not just for himself. For we're up against it, too, all in some agony or other, none of us immune, and the things to draw us are not all mean and sordid, any more than they were for him. There is nothing mean with wanting to persist, at least till the job is done or those who'll take it on are up to it. There is nothing sordid with wanting to avert a threatened city's doom, with becoming Messiah in a less grizzly fashion, with turning stones to bread, with putting God to the test, "stepping out on the promises" as they say; nothing wrong with wielding a bit of power. So in the midst of such "temptation" what to do? Begin with "Father!" "Father," he said, and even if you've nothing but the memory of a monster or mealy-mouth for a parent, you've still an inkling of the kind of freight that word should carry. "Father"—that's patience with a broad hand and a wide thumb; that's storm-windows up good and proper; that's the smell of sweat and whiskers against the cheek; that's a crack on the backsides and a new bicycle after it, love with power and muscle. That God is Father—not a deity stuck fast in old Homer's vast Empyrean, but One to whom I'm a son or daughter, loved as though I were all he had! "Father" he said—that One who came to make him known called him "Father."

Then, fired with a whole world of desire to avoid the inevitable, Jesus drew an "if" over it all—"if," he said, "if thou art willing, remove this cup." For a stoic, putting that "if" was a fairly easy matter. The stoic's cozy, little world had come tumbling down about his ears and all the power and the say-so lay with someone else, so why bother? With Jesus, it was a horse of another color. He had a hankering, that One, whatever the odds, and he let it show! When he sat down to supper with his disciples that last night he blurted out: "How I've *longed* to eat this passover with you!" And it wasn't that Jesus could sit loose because his prayer was for someone else. That'd be natural, wouldn't it, to draw the "if," to put the whole thing in the conditional form where another was involved—but unnatural for him, since what he wanted for another was all the want he had!

Perhaps, as some say, Jesus began his prayer full of hope, then broke it off. I don't know. But however he began, he ended that prayer in a "not my will, but Thine, be done." Now if you could find a man who never wanted a thing for himself, who spent every breath in his body for the other; so great and yet so gentle a man it'd tear your heart out just to hear or look at him, wouldn't that man, at some time or other, have a right to assert his own rights, even to God? Jesus did and Jesus didn't. I mean, he had the right—if ever a man had the right he did—but he didn't use it. The one true man who could stand toe to toe with the Almighty, his integrity intact, his heart pure as the day it began beating, poured his whole self on the ground there in an act of submission.

How could he do it, how could he kill the self off with a prayer like that, and what on earth for? The answer's in that "Father." The agony had to be. It was, writes Luke, a "must," for there'd be nary a "Father" for us if that Son, that incomparable Son had been without a passion. For in that agony God's fatherhood is concretized. Sometime, somewhere, that God had to come out of abstraction, break through the maybes and supposes, fix himself to a spot like this, to a man like this, so poor dumb fools like me could point and shout: "Now *there's* a Father for you!" And in that agony God's fatherhood is constituted. I mean, there was that inner necessity, that compulsion in God himself to clamber down. Because to be God, the one, true God, means to throw oneself away! Jesus bent himself beneath that will of God. But what is that will but a will to be nothing for itself, a will never to live for itself, a will to be one thing and only one—a will for us? God could not be God without being Father, and could not be Father without this agonizing Jesus in whom that fatherhood came clear!

Jesus' last night, the death all 'round and that prayer, "not my will, but thine, be done," that's the night, that's the place, that's the man, the Son in whom we've found a Father. Glory be to God!

Christ Against the Law

Pilate then called together the chief priests and the rulers and the people, and said to them, "You brought me this man as one who was perverting the people; and after examining him before you, behold, I did not find this man guilty of any of your charges against him; neither did Herod, for he sent him back to us. Behold, nothing deserving death has been done by him; I will therefore chastise him and release him." But they all cried out together, "Away with this man, and release to us Barabbas"—a man who had been thrown into prison for an insurrection started in the city, and for murder. Pilate addressed them once more, desiring to release Jesus; but they shouted out, "Crucify, crucify him!" A third time he said to them, "Why, what evil has he done? I have found in him no crime deserving death; I will therefore chastise him and release him." But they were urgent, demanding with loud cries that he should be crucified. And their voices prevailed. So Pilate gave sentence that their demand should be granted. He released the man who had been thrown into prison for insurrection and murder, whom they asked for; but Jesus he delivered up to their will. (Luke 23:13-25).

Pilate has often been painted as a combination of a Kansas City or Newark boss, the mayor of Chicago and the Godfather—a venal, bloodthirsty wretch with some trace of conscience left, to the extent he recognized Jesus' innocence and made at least a half-hearted attempt to let him go, but in the end willing to trade off the truth to keep himself in office.

Pilate, of course, used extreme measures. When he first arrived at his Jerusalem post, he sent troops with their silver eagles and images of the emperor Tiberius into the Holy City. He filched shekels from the temple treasury to build an aqueduct, and when the Jews rioted, had his plainclothesmen mill about among them and beat them to a pulp. He raised shields in honor of Caesar in Herod's own palace, and at a festival mingled the blood of Galileans with their sacrifices. A brutal attack on Samaritans at Gerizim a handful of years following Jesus' death led to his removal from office and subsequent suicide. Pilate, then, seems to have been rather a "bad egg." It's almost incredible the Ethiopian church should have hailed him as a saint for his witness to Jesus' innocence.

Thus, whenever we tell the story of Pilate, it's customary to describe him as more anxious to have done with the entire Jesusmess than with justice, and like Claggart in Melville's *Billy Budd,* both attracted and repulsed by the stunning purity of Jesus to the point where he could plead his cause and yet give him a taste of the lash and allow those second-class citizens of Jerusalem to nail him. For hundreds of years Pilate has served as symbol of the politician, anxious to keep his seat at any cost.

But we might be nearer the truth if we imagined Pilate much in the role of a police sergeant in the inner-city. Worried about his superior's estimate of his work, assigned to a high-risk area, trying to hang on till pension time and compelled to curb force or violence with the force or violence the law demands in such sticky instances. Jews in Pilate's day were not "scared of the sight of their own blood," as we used to say when I was a boy. They were a tough, grizzled and extremely inventive lot—much as the Irish Sinn Fein or the Israeli sabras of today.

Pilate had to be rough, and though a more enlightened age might describe his methods as nothing short of brutal, they did not at all differ from others of his age, not even from those of the Jews when they had the country all to themselves!

To make a long story short, there was little, if any, hanky-panky in Pilate's treatment of Jesus. There's no doubt that with the fall of his sponsor, he saw himself between the devil and the deep blue sea, would rather have avoided confrontation with his peevish subjects, but in the end he did only what Roman law required—eliminate a man who threatened the power and authority of Caesar.

And what of the Jews? If we squeeze out a bit of sympathy for Pilate, aren't we obliged to take out after them, damn them as the true instigators, the authentic crucifiers of the Lord? Since the day Christ left the womb he'd been badgered and hounded and harried and harassed, plotted against, scorned, disbelieved and even libelled by those Jews. They'd everlastingly tried to trip him up; were forever after getting the goods on him, and at his trial they hauled in false witnesses. They were a bad lot! But what should they have done with a man who implied, hinted, suggested, came flat outright and stated that what God knew he himself knew, what God did he did, what God was he was? The law was clear—Moses had said, kill him; one way or another put an end to him and string him up for all to see so the same fate didn't befall another.

Indeed, since the Jews in Pilate's day could not execute without the procurator's sanction, they were forced to suggest that Caesar wouldn't take kindly to Pilate's letting such a fellow roam free, forced to shout, as another Gospel has it, "we've no king but Caesar!" That was a bit much, but no more than when Christian folks nowadays aver they've no head, no chief, no boss but the President. People have been heard to say as much in church. And, as for the false witnesses, their testimony was thrown out of court, and Jesus indicted on his own say-so. Earlier that morning they had asked him, "Are you the Son of God, then?" and he replied, "You say that I am," or as Mark reports,

"I am; and you will see the Son of man sitting at the right hand of Power, and coming with the clouds of heaven!" For the Jews, their law was as clear as Pilate's. There was little hanky-panky in their treatment of Jesus.

But if both Pilate and the Jews behaved in more or less legal and appropriate fashion, how fix the blame for Jesus' death? If we can't pin it on some bloodsucking Roman turned cautious or on a murderous gang of Jews, where then, on whom?

The world you and I live in is a world regulated by law—good law, bad law, indifferent law—but law nonetheless. If any of us were to attempt something we oughtn't or we're not, we'd meet the law head on. The law reads we're to behave in a certain manner, do certain things and refrain from others. When we exceed the limit, we come up against the law. When we attempt to do or say something for which we've no credentials, we come hard against the law. Show me a healer or educator who hasn't suffered shipwreck on the law once he's tried his hand at winding generators without the training for it. Or show me a garage repairman who hasn't gone aground once he's taken a shine to doctoring without a license. Not merely thieves and rapists and pushers encounter the law head on—each of us is bounded, limited by law, law in a thousand different shapes and sizes. Even the anarchist, even the man or woman who's attempted to get free of the legal, one way or another finds himself under law if he's to survive. And what's more, we find our self-justification in the law. You've got a union card, a Ph.D. or a driver's license or a Bank America card—the signal or symbol of your right to drive a truck, teach, or charge a noon lunch. So it's not merely that our existence is inextricably bound up with law —from law we derive our right to be what we are, to do what we do—in law we find our self-justification.

Now, when grace enters such a setting, when it makes its

entry into such a world, when unbounded love and compassion, when God makes his descent into such a context, the context of law, the only thing waiting for him is crucifixion. For grace and Christ have nothing in common with law, with existence oriented to law and hence with man's self-justification, nothing to do with life as it is. So of what use would it have been for Christ to speak out, to protest his innocence? By law he was guilty!

It was God who first gave the law; out of love for his creation he gave it so we wouldn't tear one another to shreds. But it was to *us* he gave it, creatures unable to use it for anything else than our own justification. There's scarcely been a soul who's used the law, obeyed the law, kept the law, observed the law, assented to the law for any other reason. And for that reason law can never yield what the God who revealed himself in Jesus is in a hot sweat to give—his grace and his love!

However this word may jar you, however many questions it might raise, if you cannot see the difference between grace and law, between Christ and Moses and Pilate and the Magna Charta and the Constitution and Bill of Rights; if you can't perceive the unbelievable disparity, the incredible distance between them; can't see that what he is will not mix, mesh or harmonize with whatever limits us and by which we seek to justify ourselves or interpret our right to exist, you're lost to grace, to God!

The Christian community, the church, that noble army of men and boys, matrons and maids is not a society of do-gooders or law-keepers within the vortex of a corrupt and decadent world, but rather an ensign, a beacon announcing the advent of something entirely and radically new, the entry in Jesus Christ of something not reckoned or measured by what a man does or does not do, a grace on which not one creature has a lien or can make a claim, grace, sheer, pure grace—a new aeon, a new life, a new existence, a new world charged and filled by the Spirit of that Jesus who once stood mute and silent before Pilate and the Jews.

It was the law that killed Jesus, not merely Pilate or a few hundred Hebrews. It was law, your law, my law, everybody's law—and it couldn't have been otherwise. For law measures, but love and grace do not; law bounds and limits but love and grace set free; law requites wrong for wrong and right for right, but love gives and forgives and without reason; law is man's justifier, but grace is God's justice.

Not because of Pilate, then, but because human existence is what it is, a tangle of law, and you and I its users who raise our claims by it, because of us, Christ died. There's none of us can't sing, "I it was denied Thee, I crucified Thee"! Now, if only I could move you to believe that it was not against us that he died, but rather for us! That would mean an end to life by law!

And the Word Became Flesh

(Christmas)

And the Word became flesh and dwelt among us, full of grace and truth; we have beheld his glory, glory as of the only Son from the Father. (John 1:14)

"And the Word became flesh." The word hurled itself into a world of words, good words, poor words, words with meaning, words without, words scarcely used, words never used, words used up and mouthed to death, words like "wonderful," "beautiful," "colossal," "I love you," and "go to grass!" It squeezed its way into the dictionary between "Worcestershire sauce" and "worm." Now why couldn't that which came a-catapulted into this world of words have been something else? At least *another* word! Why that word "word" which means anything—talk, conversation, chatter, prattle, palaver, blarney, hocus pocus—and therefore nothing? Yes, indeed, the Word of God and all of that. "And God said, 'Let there be light,' and there was light" and all of that. Genesis one and all of that. The Logos, the Stoics, Alexandria, Philo and all of that. The sound of it may once have made the Jew or Greek giddy, made him feel as though he were teetering on the jaws of God. But after nineteen centuries a poor thing—needing etymology and philology and lexicography and historiography and imagining and whispering and shouting and ringing of bells and the sign of the cross and music and tapers

and playing of lights and chasubles and incense and a pretty
blonde in the choir. What a poor thing that "word" is!
  Some have attempted a substitute.

> Blest Christmas morn, though murky clouds
> Pursue thy way,
> Thy light was born where storm enshrouds
> Nor dawn nor day!

> Dear Christ, forever here and near,
> No cradle song,
> No natal hour and mother's tear,
> To thee belong.

> Thou God-idea, Life-encrowned,
> The Bethlehem babe
> Beloved, replete, by flesh embound
> Was but thy shade!

The twentieth century female counterpart of Marcion from
Sinope who wrote this stanza couldn't stand to have him shivering there in any dictionary, wrapping himself with articles and
particles and prepositions to keep warm. He had to be some
other word, at least, some big, grandiose word, some high-
falutin' word, some heaven-smashing, earth-embracing, unde-
finable, uncontainable word, gloriously, snobbishly unable to
traffic with nouns like "shepherd" or "cradle," or "cow" or
"stable." A nineteenth century American scholar toyed with
terms such as "thought" and "soul" and "principle of order."
"In the beginning was Thought. Thought belonged to God.
Thought was in nature divine. . . . In the beginning was Soul.
Soul was inherent in God. Soul was in nature divine. . . . And
the principle of order became flesh and dwelt among us." And
after the scholar's death, his publisher wrote: "In view of Pro-

fessor ————————'s own uncertainty and the limitations which translation places upon interpretation, it has seemed wise to use the untranslatable 'Logos' in the text." "In the beginning was the Logos. . . . And the Logos became flesh . . ."

Oh, it's translatable enough. But who wants just "word"? Why not "idea," a whole system of ideas, an architectonic of thought? Or, at any rate, if a word, a word with a modifier, like "good word." "What's the good word?" they say. Or if that sound must stand alone and solitary, then let it appear with a capital W! This discontents you—you want to jump up from your seat now and yell: "But this word is the 'Very Word of God—the Word of Beginning and End, of the Creator and Redeemer, of Judgment and Righteousness. . . .' When confronted by this Word, 'human lips and ears must display their inadequacy,' by it the church is established and broken in pieces, a Word of 'blessed terribleness by which men are related to God.'" You may want to interrupt with a hymn: "O Word of God Incarnate, O Wisdom from on high!" or perhaps with a line from Athanasius: "The incorporeal, incorruptible, immaterial Word of God entered our world. . . ."

I love all those lines too, but they are only an anointing for burial, a sweet incense which in the end will not stay the odor of decay. The word has been taxed beyond enduring, exhausted, spent, used up. It was inevitable. To come as one word among many other words—that was one thing. But to come only as word, as word alone, that made its death and burial inevitable. It could claim things. It could claim to be *the* word, the word of which all others are only the refraction. It could claim to be the eternal Yea and Nay, in face of which any other yes or no is silenced and dumb. But the moment its sound was heard, it was inevitable that it should be fixed there, nailed there between "Worcestershire sauce" and "worm," a thing to be blankly stared

at, ambiguous, a question mark, suffering a Heinz 57 varieties of
interpretation, scorned, spurned, or worse, missed, skipped over
in men's haste to get at other words, other sounds—sounds like
"work" or "world."

Not only was all this inevitable. This was the intention!
Whatever there was of God, whatever there was of reality, all
became a cipher, a datum in a dictionary; whatever there was of
beauty, truth and goodness all became a sound to be muttered
by babes, a thing to be hideously mispronounced by posturing
fools, to be used for lack of a "better" word, to be tossed away
unuttered like half-eaten, rotten fruit in favor of some other
golden phrase—for us!

Put up the trees, throw on the tinsel, pass the pipe and the
bowl, sing "Fa-la-la," stuff the turkey, pile the room high with
the boughten gifts, feel munificent, beneficent, magnanimous and
magnificent, shed a tear, read Dickens, leave an empty chair, buy
seals, go to church at midnight and you'll never in all this world
tidy up what he has become for us—a plain, ordinary, hum-drum
word that never takes vacation from its monotony, from its per-
petually being born, dying and being buried each time a man
opens his mouth. We're always after trumpet blasts, and Hallelujah choruses and whirring wings. In Rainer Maria Rilke's ode
to the night of Christ's birth the angels say to Mary: "You ex-
pected more than this"? "Look!" we yell, "the God-idea's coming. Where in thunder are those angels! C'mon Gabriel, you and
Michael first, then the rest of you—Uriel, Ariel and whatcha-
callit. Now remember, just fifteen feet off the ground and hover-
ing. Shepherds! Shepherds put those sandwiches away and kneel!
Magi, suck in your cheeks and look haggard—you've just been
on a long trip! Somebody get Joseph out of the delivery room,
and shoo those goats out of here! Remember, when you hear him

bawl, all together on the count of three—'Silent Night, Holy Night.' Now where's Gruber?"

But it won't work; it won't wash. For who can feel the heartbeat of an idea which presses against the womb; who can give a thought breasts to tug; who can clasp the fingers and toes of a God-idea; who can crucify a principle of order? But a word, this word, though inevitably to be spurned and scorned because it willed to be, loved to be—this word is something to be heard, to be perceived, to be felt, to be clasped to one's breast, clung to, obeyed, hidden away in the mind, uttered in a moment of despair, shouted in a minute of triumph, whispered in the hour of death, and this word is mine!

The message of Christmas is that God has turned to us as word, to be rolled about on the tongue, to suffer injustice appropriate to its pitiful plainness, but nonetheless to be our own, relentlessly, persistently our very own—for our loving or our abandoning, for our uttering or our leaving unuttered, for our embracing or thrusting aside. And even though there should be other sounds, other gods to become other words, more golden words, perhaps, more contenting, grander—when I took this one word I had already left behind whatever others there may be. This one word has been enough—I have no room for any other. And I know that when all other words in the book have lost mouths to speak them, this one solitary word will still be sounded true and clear, for "the grass withers, the flower fades; but the word of our God will stand forever!"

Why?

For God sent the Son into the world, not to condemn the world, but that the world might be saved through him. (John 3:17)

Now this word ought to be heard again, and with both ears. It's a truth that has got to get out again. For with everything else that's gone wrong, few seem to remember *why* in the world God took it into his head to send Jesus.

For most, I'll wager, Jesus is still that scowling, beetle-browed Christus Pantocrator the Byzantines used to paint on the ceilings of their churches. Remember? He's the goblin who'll get ya if ya don't watch out, who'll throw 'way down the stairs all the kids who never say their prayers. One way or another, Jesus is still a synonym for judgment. And that's one of the reasons little boys whose whiskered, warted aunts threatened he'd never love them if they were naughty grew up to be theologians who railed at what they termed the "exclusivistic claim" made on Jesus' behalf, who called those who appeared to discover something infinitely more "binitarians" or "Christological unitarians," and in general tried to make God look good without Jesus.

It's no wonder, of course, what with every collection of humans imaginable insisting he came to espouse their cockeyed schemes and send everybody else packing. When I was about thirteen, some middle-aged, pious sex pervert accosted me on a frightfully long bridge across the Illinois river and asked me if I were saved, ready to violate me and throw me into the drink if I said no. I think if he'd been the only man I'd ever seen, I could have

ended up writing the piece that got that German theologian so
much news: *Muss man an Jesus glauben wenn man an Gott
glauben will?*—"Must we believe in Jesus if we want to believe
in God?" "Goodness me, no!" At any rate, Jesus still remains a
principle of exclusion, and it's no wonder.

But why did he come? Why did God send him? "That the
world might be saved," the Good Book says. God wanted the
whole wide world to be free for him and for every living creature under heaven. So he sent Jesus, lowly born, stomach empty
from forgetting to eat—what with the need and pain of the
world and all—hands nailed to a tree, Jesus of Nazareth, dead
and risen.

How could folks make such an error as to think he came for
any other reason than to make us free, caged and helpless as we
were? I know, I'm not taking men's capacity for abysmal evil
seriously when I imagine that if only the world knew *why,* every
mother's son would make his heart a throne for that humble
king. For some *won't* be free, and they won't have others free.
But that's scarcely a reason for blaming the One who's willed
nothing but our deliverance since time began. And I know, too,
that some want freedom when and where they please, and think
God's choice of Jesus as the occasion for the world's salvation
smacks of a royal and sovereign decree, and they'll have none
of that.

But isn't there a kind of sovereignty in every event, isn't there
a kind of once-for-allness in anything that occurs in our world?
Shoot an arrow from a bow—can you wish it back? If the love
of God was to be seen, embraced and loved in turn, how else
but in an event which, like every other, should share in once-for-
allness, in the non-repeatable, in the historical? If to be human
means to affirm our own life as a life in space and time, finite
and temporal, can it be something less than human to affirm

that history, that event, that life, that beautiful life in which God's infinite love became concrete? Or, do you suppose you are a god, you, with your nose high in the air?

Jesus came down to us men, not to gods, and he came to save, to ransom, to deliver, to set us free! "Glorioso!" as Little Orphan Annie used to say. That's the reason why, there's no other. That word, that good old word's enough to give you gooseflesh the rest of the day!

The Justice of God

(Reformation Day)

But now the righteousness of God has been manifested apart from law, although the law and the prophets bear witness to it, the righteousness of God through faith in Jesus Christ for all who believe. For there is no distinction; since all have sinned and fall short of the glory of God, they are justified by his grace as a gift, through the redemption which is in Christ Jesus, whom God put forward as an expiation by his blood, to be received by faith. This was to show God's righteousness, because in his divine forbearance he had passed over former sins; it was to prove at the present time that he himself is righteous and that he justifies him who has faith in Jesus. Then what becomes of our boasting? It is excluded. On what principle? On the principle of works? No, but on the principle of faith. For we hold that a man is justified by faith apart from works of law. (Romans 3:21-28)

"Justice." That word conjures up a courtroom scene, a bench and a judge; an attorney for the defense, for the prosecution, and witnesses for both. You see a jury, and high above the jurist's bench some kind of symbol to represent the thing gives force and meaning to the whole affair—the rule of law. Do you remember the figure of justice with her flaming sword, of "blind" justice with her balance, her scales? That sword and those scales represent law. For, as we commonly think or talk of it, there's no justice which isn't somehow set in the context of law, a law "on" or "off" the books, a law codified and written down, or a law deep in the heart of a man. One reason that word "justice" still has some starch to it is that most folks have a pretty fair notion of what it means, and what it means always has something to do with law, "on" or "off" the books.

Now, when it's a question of the justice or righteousness of God, it's a horse of another color. For God's justice has nothing to do with law, nothing to do with law "on" or "off" the books—the Ten Commandments, say, or the moral law. That doesn't mean God doesn't care a fig for law, that he doesn't take seriously the ethical situation or that people who believe in God are a passel of libertines who do whatever they jolly well please. It means only that the justice of God has nothing to do with law. It wasn't "revealed," as St. Paul puts it, in any Perry Mason courtroom.

Letting that truth penetrate your heart and mind won't be easy. For one thing, you mastered your do's and don'ts when you were quite small, and when it finally came time to hear of the justice of God, you'd pretty much made up your mind God was a kind of celestial banker with whom you did business on a tit for tat basis, and his justice took on all the earmarks of a medal for bravery. And, letting that truth penetrate your heart and mind won't be easy because you're fairly comfortable with the legal end of things now. Whatever rules you've laid down for yourself you've more or less satisfied—giving an employer an honest day's labor; teaching a full schedule; keeping a neat house; refraining from murder, rapine and blatant dishonesty. You've satisfied the law, your law, somebody's law, and your conscience is quite at ease. It's like taking a cold bath to hear that God's justice has nothing whatever to do with law. And I don't think I'd care to tell you that's so, if it weren't there in black and white in St. Paul, plain as the nose on your face: "But now the righteousness of God has been manifested apart from the law." And what of all the good you've done? Like giving your employer an honest day's labor, teaching a full schedule, keeping a neat house and what-not? Well, it wouldn't be true to say all that was a waste of time, to say with one old church father that all that good was nothing but a "shining vice." Be thankful for everything good, even if done by a flaming Muslim or an atheist! It's just that where God's justice is concerned, God's righteousness, we're all beggars, with nothing to trade. And the reason why is that he's not a storekeeper, he's a giver! He's not operating a market which requires life and time congealed into cold, hard cash; he's not running a bank needs collateral. He's after giving what he's got away! That's true of just about anything you can say of God. God is love, we're told, but his love is there only to make us lovely. God is all-powerful, but his power is there only to make us strong. God is holy, but his holiness is there only to make us saints. The same is true of his justice. It's there and he's got it, but he possesses it only to make us just, to put us right with himself and with everybody else under the sun. He's a giver!

A giver, of course, gives on his own terms. A man doesn't pick the time and place in which someone gives him a gift. Oh yes, couples about to marry sometimes leave a note with the jeweler to the effect that if friends inquire, they'll take stainless steel in the drooping petunia pattern, thank you. I've never quite been able to warm to that type procedure, but even there the giver sets the time and place. There's a bit of sovereignty in any kind of giving, and you oughtn't balk at allowing God the same courtesy you give your great aunt Millie.

Now the time, the year, the day, the place, the occasion, the event, the man in whom God gives us his justice is Jesus Christ.

I grant you, it's a strange place to find the justice of God—in that "worm" of a man, born to a little nobody, suckled in a rude stable, with less than a bird or fox could call home, nailed by all those good church people to a cross. It's absurd that the justice of God should be on display in a travesty of human justice, in a miserable act of wrong; that it should all boil down to that lonely, helpless man hanging there and crying, "My God, my God, why hast thou forsaken me?"

I find it strange, don't you, that God's justice should appear under the sign of its opposite, strange that the love of God should be in what's unlovely, the power of God in what's powerless, the mercy and forgiveness of God in a merciless and vengeful deed? Of course, if I were God, I would never have fixed on such a spot—never in a million years! With me, it would have been smoke and lightning bolts and giant letters in the sky and earthquakes and armies and battles and myself standing on Mt. Everest roaring, "I'm God and here's justice, and I'll huff and I'll puff and I'll blow your house down!" It *is* absurd that God should be what and where and how no one expects him to be, that his justice which should be bright and shining for us all to see, should be where we can only see its opposite.

But the absurdity of God only answers to our own. We think there's justice in the handbook for local No. 309 or in Moses or a Harvard philosopher or our own candidate for president. We look for it there, when we know, deep down to the marrow of our bones that whatever justice these things promise is bound, like Cinderella at midnight, to change back into its opposite! Show me a justice, show me *your* justice which isn't a deep, dark wrong for someone else! God's absurdity only answers to our own, but where we change justice to wrong, power to impotence and love to hate, he turns wrong, impotence and hate to justice, power and love in Jesus Christ!

Do you remember how he was with children; do you recall what he did for the sick and the hungry; do you recollect his infinite patience with those who never understood him; do you remember how he forgot himself; how he loved? Great heaven, how he loved! Mightn't it be, mightn't it just be that in the absurd, miserable fate of that One, pinned to the wood like a butterfly in a collector's case, the justice to end all justice, the justice which is the origin and source, the Itasca headwaters of every just thought and deed in the whole wide world has appeared?

God played grandpa, he played doting grandpa with the whole human race, just peeking at its foibles and crimes through his fingers, until *he* came, and there, in him, God not only "showed" his justice—what a paltry thing that word "show" is when we're talking of something in which God poured out his whole soul—he "proved" it! Not in a thundering from Sinai; not in the rhetoric of a Pericles on some Athenian hill; not from the Roman forum, but in Jesus of Nazareth, humble and lowly. And if the church calls itself by the name of that ex-monk is anything more than a mere denomination, clutching its investments like a skirt in a high wind, it's because, with that whirlwind from Wittenberg, it sees in Jesus Christ the very justice of God, clings to him for dear life, sees God first and above all there, and once having seem him there can see him at the end of a rope. And if it doesn't; if it can't see God's own justice there, then better to give the dog a bad name and hang it.

That word "all" at the tag end of our pledge of allegiance— "with liberty and justice for all" has a hollow ring to it, for the dirt-poor, say, or for folks with the wrong color skin, or for boys who can't afford college, or for children and old women who have nothing to "tool" down a free-way with or put in a car park. It's been said that the law, any law, and hence whatever liberty

or justice it guarantees, is always on the side of the possessor,
the owner. With us, then, that word "all" is hyperbole, it's an
exaggeration or at best an ideal. There are even fascist states
where a visitor can't keep his own, miserable beard and get
through customs. But *his* "all" is an honest-to-God, cross-my-
heart-and-hope-to-die "all"! *His* justice is for all, "since all have
sinned and fall short of the glory of God." Now that last word's
not meant to be a "hooker" or curve ball; it's not meant to set up
a principle of exclusion—unless, of course, you consider yourself
trustworthy, loyal, obedient, cheerful, friendly, helpful, courteous,
kind, thrifty, brave, clean, reverent twenty four hours a day,
which is just about the most ridiculous thing I've ever heard—
it's meant to comfort all us poor, ornery people with the everlasting good news that God's justice is for us, not for giants or angels; for us who're all in the same kettle of fish, turning love to
hate, power to impotence and right to wrong. Over the gate to
his justice he hasn't written, "Enter, you pure, chaste, uncon-
taminated hunk of human being"; he's written "for all, for sinners," and it's all the same, all the same.

But if God's justice is for all, all of God is in that justice! What
God did there in Jesus wasn't something he managed with a
flick of the wrist. He gave *himself* there, so that getting justice
from him is nothing more or less than getting Jesus Christ as gift,
for it's in that man that all the treasures and grandeur of God
are hid and tucked away. You've heard that word "justification"
a time or two, and till now it may have been nothing but a
meaningless abstraction. Well, bless your heart, it means nothing
at all if it doesn't mean getting God's own very self in Jesus
Christ as a gift. And when someone gives you his whole, almighty self, with nothing of him left over to wonder about,
nothing of himself left to slip away like an extra piece of dough
cut away from the pie, then it's all over with playing store, and

you've nothing to give him back but love and trust! Now, that's what it means to be "justified" by faith. See, what a glorious Gospel this is, and what a magnificent God he is who gives us all he is and has, and for whom we've nothing at all to give but only what *all* can give—our love and our trust. "But now the righteousness of God has been manifested apart from law . . . the righteousness of God through faith in Jesus Christ for all who believe. . . ."

To Those Who Are Called

(Ordination)

> For Jews demand signs and Greeks seek wisdom, but we preach Christ crucified, a stumbling block to Jews and folly to Gentiles, but to those who are called, both Jews and Greeks, Christ the power of God and the wisdom of God (1 Corinthians 1:22-24).

The way to manage a piece of super-market hamburger or any other indigestible item is to splash it with A-1 sauce or ketchup and smother it with onions and mushrooms. Now, someone's been squirting one condiment or other on this text since the day it was written—so as to make it edible. If Columbus discovered whatever in the world it was he discovered for the sake of improving Ferdinand and Isabella's lunch, much of that company calls itself after the name of Christ has exhausted whole centuries of its life on a hunt for something to "tenderize" these tough, gristly words. "We preach Christ crucified!" wrote Paul. That's scarcely a tempting tid-bit for anyone inside or outside the Church.

So, the trick has been to package this raw stuff prettily and con the public into buying it with a few Madison Avenue clichés like, "it tastes so good, and it's so good for you!" When Lord Gordon saw what Roman Catholics and the Eastern Orthodox and Copts had done with that spot where Christ was nailed, how they'd raised up that Byzantine thing-a-ma-jig over it, and filled every little nook and cranny with the cloying stench of incense, he romped about Jerusalem for weeks, looking for another spot still retained a bit of romance and now, trips to the Holy Land include a look-see at "Gordon's Calvary," led by devoutly lisping, pretty Dutch girls. So if you're all for the icons and the candles and the mummery, off to the Church of the Holy Sepulchre! If not, take a walk to the other place with all the flowers and trees. But it all comes round to the same thing. Ketchup and onions! Both spots serve as symbol of what's happened to this word of the apostle and the event to which it points.

But what if that event were understood? What if "The Old Rugged Cross," "In the Cross of Christ I Glory" and all the rest were denuded of the million and one associations they conjure up —Susie in her white, baptismal dress, "mewling and puking" in her mother's arms; Johnny standing tall and pimply at confirmation; Sunday dinner at Grandma's and after it a John Wayne matinee; preachers with their impeccable rhetoric and churches with vaulted naves and flying buttresses; flags in chancels, "God Bless Our Native Land" and "confound our enemies"; lutefisk and bratwurst in the church parlors; the stations of the cross; priests and professors in their regalia; Billy Graham before the uncounted masses; MacLaughlin in the White House and Hal Lindsey with his super-keen moustache—what if the whole pretentious flummery made to swirl about that cross were suddenly swept away and all that remained was to point to it and to that awful thing hanging on it, with nary a scrap to cover its nakedness? That'd be a different story. Yet it's to that, precisely and only to that you've sworn yourself!

Some folks, of course, want signs. "Show us a sign!" cried Jesus' countrymen, "some proof you've really come from God!" Folks now want signs just as badly, and not only from the hucksters of anti-perspirant ads ("if you're like most people, your left arm will convince your right arm"). They want evidence that truth won't forever be on the scaffold and wrong forever on the throne, some little proof that behind the dim unknown there's God, still keeping watch. And others are after a bit of wisdom, something to catch up all the pain and agony in an intelligible scheme, tidy up the chaos they live in. And when you lump them all together—folks who hanker after signs and folks who hanker after wisdom—you've ninety-nine and forty-four one hundredths percent of all the creatures on this planet. And all you've got for them is the scandal and folly of a crucified Jesus! On the Palatine at Rome, there's an ancient graffito scratched into the rock— a crucified figure with the head of an ass and beneath it the inscription: "Alexamenos prays to his god." That thing is over a thousand years old, but it expresses the disgust men and women still feel once they understand what's afoot with the Christian faith.

The fact is, you're an atheist, in the classical, first century sense of the term, for in midst of all this clamoring for proofs and explanations and solutions and rationales and demonstrations, you've only the story of a man forsaken and abandoned by God and man, the story of a crucified God. I expect you're some worse off than the ordinary, plain vanilla atheist. He, at least, has some ideology or perspective by which to judge time and human events —his precious dialectic, say. And the materialist has his creed— "plenty of hard work, boy, plenty of elbow grease and you'll make it to the top"—he has his bundle of green stuff to bow down to, and it's something he can see. But all you can muster is a call to hang between heaven and hell with Jesus of Nazareth there, and without a single shred of evidence or explanation for your insistence that that broken man is where the power and wisdom of God belong!

A group ought to think twice before it heaps up brick and

mortar for a church and raises a cross above some marble slab; a bishop ought to think twice before he lets it dangle over his paunch, for that cross is one great, thundering, ear-splitting "No!" to everything we naturally conceive God to be, to every impulse we call noble or righteous or good. It indicts everything which passes with us for good taste, breeding, piety or even religion. That cross which once stood "outside the camp" as the Book of Hebrews has it— let it find its way to a thousand sanctuaries; let the crude and splintered wood find its substitute in some gorgeous piece of bronze or gold—it still spells the reversal of every human value.

For one thing, anyone who thinks about God, thinks of might, of omnipotence, of a Being who holds this spinning orb like a tiny top in his grand, majestic paw, but that figure on the tree couldn't even help himself! Some who taunted him on that grim Friday may once have been believers. They may once have seen some sudden burst of glory in him, but after watching him dangle on the wood, suffered a violent shipwreck of their dream and in blind despair yelled: "If you're the Christ, save yourself and us!" Yet the word of Paul and every other blessed writer of the New Testament is that this wretched scene has cut time and history into two pieces as a birthday child cuts its cake, that because of this miserable death everything has changed—life has changed, the world has changed, the entire twinkling and blinking cosmos has changed, and heaven and earth locked into a new phase which races toward some incredible goal, and all because of this suffering Jesus! It's a reversal, but who can see it? Where's the proof or where's the wisdom in a God's peeling off his pomp and grandeur in hunger and thirst and wounds and sighs?

And, if it were possible to conceive of a God as dying, it might make all the difference if that death were for someone noble, but the word is that this God was crucified not for the wise, mighty or well born, but for the foolish, weak, low and despised. One thing you'll have to give him, hanging there between two thieves and executed like a common thug—his death was altogether consistent with his life. He'd consorted with outcasts, cripples and whores, badgering men who'd made good by dint of sheer, moral effort and flogging nice people out of their church. But it's all still a reversal! For where's the sign or where's the sense in a God whom ancient seers and prophets heralded as too holy for a man to look upon, whose sacred fire no one could touch except on pain of death, throwing aside his scruples in this man and come to rock all weary and ornery flesh in his arms, like a mother her child?

There's no sign, and there's no sense, "but to those who are called," and that means you, the word of that cross is enough to burst a man's heart and brain with hope! For if it is so that God behaves in this fashion, contrary to all human value and expectation, then there's more to your world than you can see, more to your own life than you can see. Then the pain and anguish and doubt sure to fill your days, the torture at not knowing whether you've got hold of the deity or the devil, the inability to pray without the suspicion your words have gone no further than the ceiling of your room, the monotony and drudgery of what some love to call "this glorious profession," then all that is nothing but the mask behind which lurks Someone working to shape you and everything that is into something new! If it's so that God acts under the sign of his opposite, if he's chosen what's foolish in the world to shame the wise, what's weak to bully the strong, what's mean and low, even things that aren't, to bring to nothing things that are, so that no human being might boast in his presence, then you're free of every proposition, theorem or scheme under the sun, free of what for others must count as religion, morality and law; free of every human court, free to love as he did, free to live and die as he did. Remember old Martin's word? "Des Christen Herz auf Rosen geht, wenn's mitten unterm Kreuze steht"—"the Christian's heart walks upon roses when it stands beneath the cross." Take your stand there, too, for God did not leave him forsaken and abandoned! He raised him up, raised him to be both Lord and Christ! *Therefore,* "we preach Christ crucified"—not signs, not warrantees, not wisdom, not a rationale, but Christ crucified, "to those who are called, both Jews and Greeks, the power and wisdom of God!"

For Us There Is One God

Yet for us there is one God, the Father, from whom are all things and for whom we exist, and one Lord, Jesus Christ, through whom are all things and through whom we exist. (1 Corinthians 8:6).

Suppose the things we see—tables and chairs, buildings and books—aren't real at all. Suppose whatever we think about, the content of our consciousness, is nothing but a reflection of things that aren't there in still another non-existent thing—our brain. Suppose then, that our life, our world and everything in it is nothing but one grand illusion we've somehow conjured up to get along. Not many Anglo-Saxons have taken to this notion, though a good many Germans have. The history of thought has been a kind of see-saw Margery Daw on this issue, with one side tipping the other off the teeter-totter, and vice versa.

Now Paul didn't much care for the purely formal discussion of what is and what isn't and how we tell the one from the other. But he took a hard line on two things which have discombobulated thinkers on either side of the aisle. The first is that whatever exists has its origin and its destiny in God. Tricycles, bathtubs, lunar modules and the minds which conceive them; calculus, logarythms and the laws of thought; love, laughter, human intimacy, pain, suffering and death—they all begin and end with God. "From him are all things and for him we exist," said Paul.

The second thing on which Paul took a hard line is that nothing came into being, nothing at all, and nothing will get to its destination; nothing comes from God and nothing will get to

God apart from the instrumentality of the life of that one, lone man in that one lone place from that one lone time—Jesus of Nazareth. Shoes and ships and sealing wax, cabbages and kings; poetry and polyphonic, babies and polliwogs—without him nothing was made that was made. "One Lord, Jesus Christ, through whom are all things and through whom we exist," said Paul.

In these two things, in this ancient creed—some of which Paul got from others, and some of which he penned himself—is distilled whatever that gloriously obnoxious little Jew ever said or did. Everything begins and ends with God, and everything that begins and ends with God begins and ends through Jesus Christ—that's Paul, that's pure Paul, melted down, to the irreducible core of him. What's left is only commentary, more frosting on the cake.

Now, what do you think? Shall we reduce this little creed to a command? Most often the church has interpreted it as command. "You want in? Then here's what you've got to do: agree that everything starts and stops with God and starts and stops through Jesus. Otherwise, out!" The reason some of you may be crippled for the study of theology, if not for maturity plain and simple, is that you've not yet shrugged off the spectre of the legal, not yet exorcised those old ghosts forever howling rules. Well, a command is not what Paul has in mind! When he writes, "for *us* there is one God, for *us* there is one Lord," he also has it in his head to say: "Look! That One who fills the seas and tiny puddles, scoops out the valleys, tops the peaks and makes the eagles nest there, formed man and woman and all the other little beasties; that One toward whom the whole cosmos, with its stars and planets and quasars, strains like a bullet ready to leave its chamber, and that One through whom everything that is pulses and throbs with life, who came down Immanuel—that One is for us! He's for us!"

So that "for us" doesn't merely mean "where we're concerned," though it may mean that first of all. It also means that "on our account," "for our sakes," "on our behalf," "for us," there's that one God and that one Lord.

Now if that's so, if he's for us, then everything that begins and ends with him, and everything that begins and ends through him—and what's left, pray tell?—it's all ours! The world and life and death and the present and the future—it's all ours, because it's his, he's its origin and its fate, he's its means, its vehicle, and he's for us! Some fellow, that Paul! Some creed! Some God!

Letter and Spirit

Our sufficiency is from God, who has qualified us to be ministers of a new covenant, not in a written code but in the Spirit; for the written code kills but the Spirit gives life. (2 Corinthians 3:5b-6)

Once in a Baltimore address, Abe Lincoln talked about a law, some eighty years old, and in a way reminiscent of the ancient Jew. He was sweet and gentle about it, said mothers ought to breathe reverence for it into their babes, linked liberty to it, fixed hope for all the world to it. Like the ancient Jew. And he said later this place, this land was the "last, best hope of earth" because of it. Like the ancient Jew! But who'd talk about law now with such an infinite tenderness? We're a long way from Baltimore or Mt. Sinai, and there's nothing to do for it.

Begin with Moses, begin with Jefferson and Adams so sweetly, ever so sweetly, sing "O how I love Thy law!" or "Confirm thy soul in self control, thy liberty in law," and some day, as sure as God made little green apples, the whole thing'll get out of tune. Some day, some poor wretch will fall in love with it, and with nary a thought for what or Who it meant to echo he'll begin to call it "mine"—isn't that what they said: *"We have a law, and by that law he ought to die"*?—he'll begin to "keep" it, build a fence around it, get up a party and crucify Christ with it. Or, he'll make it his enemy; he'll summon up a colossal hate for it, resist it, revolt against it, throttle it, poke holes in it, break it, get more to do the same and breed a race of Barabbases in the doing. Find a man who isn't crazy for the law or from the law, who doesn't eat and sleep and dream it, either to use it to keep what he's got or to break it because it doesn't get him what he wants, and he'll be a strange, single, solitary kind of man.

What makes every "sweet land of liberty" turn sour? What spawns hard hats and leftists, repression and anarchy? It's not the law as such; as such law doesn't tend to rot and stink. And it's useless to talk for or against its abolition—because it's *there,* it's always *been* and it'll always be. Try doing without it; try doing without the law of your physical organism, say, and you'll croak from acute retention! The prophet had a nicer way to put it: "Can you plow the sea with oxen?" Law is there, like Everest, and you can't wish it away. But—and here's the reason why it always kills—it makes a pact, strikes a treaty, enters into an alliance with the self, the "I." And because the self's never in love with anyone or anything but itself—keeps law for itself, breaks law for itself—law begets anger and hate and dread and despair and death. Law is inevitable, but so is the death it brings. It's there, but it kills, every time—persons, communities, nations —every time. And there's no more poignant illustration of that truth now than our own "sweet land."

What's to say to a race of lawyers like ours? About all that once was noble, good and true, now gone sour on human existence? What's to say to all this "there oughta be a law, about population, procreation, pollution, poverty, penury, perversion, pornography, pusillanimous pip-squeaks and Panthers"? "God has qualified us to be ministers of a new covenant . . . in the Spirit . . . [who] gives life"! That's to say! Life from all this death by law, kept or broken, that's to say, a waiver of all my "rights"; with the "me" and "mine" clean gone out of it and nothing but a qualification to serve the new, none to love now but God and the other! That's to say! And all as *gift,* from him,

and so *every* man's possibility, *every* man's freedom, *every* man's
life

Maybe you won't see it; maybe you'll get that neurotic crack
between your eyes deeper and deeper over this rule and that,
waiting till someone kicks you in the teeth and completes the
circle, and tells you the freedom you legislated for yourself is
his slavery. But then again, maybe you will; maybe you'll waken
to the tyranny of your self and surrender it, fling it away and
come alive in the Spirit of Christ Jesus who sets us free from
the law of sin and death! That will mean a kind of death too, but
its sting is gone.

Don't perform heroics, just give yourself up! Life needn't be
one everlasting round of counterfeit hope and death by law.
Give yourself to God, and give life to the world, give hope and
love, give the new to the world! "Our sufficiency is from God,
who has qualified us to be ministers of a new covenant, not in
a written code but in the Spirit; for the written code kills, but
the Spirit gives life!"

He's Made Me His Own

Indeed I count everything as loss because of the surpassing worth of knowing Christ Jesus my Lord. For his sake I have suffered the loss of all things, and count them as refuse, in order that I may gain Christ and be found in him, not having a righteousness of my own, based on law, but that which is through faith in Christ, the righteousness from God that depends on faith; that I may know him and the power of his resurrection, and may share his sufferings, becoming like him in his death, that if possible I may attain the resurrection from the dead. Not that I have already obtained this or am already perfect; but I press on to make it my own, because Christ Jesus has made me his own. Brethren, I do not consider that I have made it my own; but one thing I do, forgetting what lies behind and straining forward to what lies ahead, I press on toward the goal for the prize of the upward call of God in Christ Jesus. (Philippians 3:8-14).

After taking four flying leaps at this text with nothing to show for it but a full wastebasket, I've decided I'm simply not up to it. And the reason is that there is nothing at all in my life or experience which can furnish any analogy to the kind of contrast Paul draws here. Aside from a few ludicrously superficial similarities, I lack everything the apostle was willing to call refuse "because of the surpassing worth of knowing Christ." With Paul, it was not at all a matter of failing at everything else and finally hitting the jackpot with Jesus, of counting as loss whatever he'd mucked up, as the English say. The man was a veritable giant—not just following his encounter with Christ, unless you assume his brain and heart and will somehow lay dormant prior to Damascus, an idea too ridiculous to contemplate. I've nothing to equal all he had and was full of joy to abandon! Nothing!

Now, I can speak of the One who claimed Paul, can say a little about the knowledge of Christ as Lord, of gaining him, being found in him and having a righteousness from God by faith—those sentences all boil down to the same thing, by the way—but lacking *both* the members in Paul's comparison, *both* the elements in the contrast, it were better for me simply to stand mute before such a text as this, or at the most exclaim, "great God in heaven! See what he had, and see what he let go!" —garbage, he called it, *skybalon,* dung, excrement—and all for the sake of sharing the suffering of Christ and the power of his resurrection!

The apostle moves on, he's not through, and that only adds to my discomfort. "Not that I have already obtained," he says. In other words, "I'm not yet at the goal; the gift God in his inestimable love has given me, is not something which cannot be lost, but must be seized ever anew, *correction,* is something which must *seize me* ever anew." I say I'm in trouble again, for if that human whirlwind, the greatest in all of Christendom considered himself far from the prize, where in the green earth am I?

Still, there is a word here to give me comfort, to set me with all the saints who've ever drawn breath, to lift me into that company thronged round the throne, a word to anoint and crown me, clad me in the purple and fix a sceptre and orb in right hand and left, and that's the word that "Christ Jesus has made me his own"! Now, that's true, that's true! I never had reason for any confidence in the flesh; as to righteousness under the law was never blameless, never had a gain worth losing, yet because Christ has made me his own, I'm suddenly toe to toe with that amazing collection of flesh and bone called Paul! I've been drawn into the sphere, toward the very center of power, greatness and true humanity, not because of what I am, have done or will do—ye gods!—but because he "has made me His own." He's given me Philippians two, the *apostolicum* and all that was so carefully put together at Nicea, Chalcedon, Augsburg and every other sacred, blessed spot for my own biography —"and being found in human form he humbled himself and became obedient unto death, even death on a cross; therefore God has highly exalted him and bestowed on him the name which is above every name"; crucified, dead, buried, risen and reigning at the right hand—that's talk, that's language about *me* now, because he has swept me up into his history, given me his life and death for my own, and set me on the way, straining toward the goal.

Brother or sister, I hope you can make a better job of it than I ever did; reach an eloquence and power of reflection which lay beyond my grasp; write a hymn, create a liturgy, shape a theology, attain to a mastery, achieve a sanctity I never could, and grand enough to set the world on its head, but without Christ's having made you his own, it will all be a nothing, fit for the heap!

Hidden History

(At the Centennial of a Former Parish)

For you have died, and your life is hid with Christ in God. (Colossians 3:3)

Paul said, "your life is hid with Christ in God." That's a funny thing to say, especially for a man whose letters are full of what our English teachers told us to keep out of ours—that "I," "I did this" or "I did that." Or did Paul mean that *your* life, *my* life are hid, but that his was an open book? Did he mean what *he* was—the greatest thinker in all Christendom—what *he* had done—propagandized the whole inhabited world—was there for everyone to see, but that only God knows what in the world the rest of us poor yokels are up to? Paul was a great many things— aggressive, obnoxious, pushy, terribly Jewish by our waspish standards, but he was never one for double standards. What he said of others he believed of himself. His life too, was hid.

Now Paul didn't live very long, and this church here is a hundred years old! So, perhaps it's an exception to Paul's rule. Didn't one of you just write its history—and I quite recall another, lengthier piece which began the history of this place with Martin Luther and ended with my sidekick! So, perhaps you're the exception—not as single bodies, but all together, with grandpa and grandma thrown in? You've put up stone and mortar, raised altars, built classrooms for your children, added heads, whole family units to your rolls, called one preacher after another, poured out hundreds of thousands of dollars for the mission of the church—and in the doing given every Scotsman, Greek and Irishman in town reason for revising his opinion of third generation immigrants. The whole thing's as hidden as a lighthouse beam!

It's still hidden, for all that, still hidden. And part of the proof is whatever anyone's been here, done here, is capable of a thousand and one interpretations. Suppose your history were to be interpreted as an attempt on the part of newcomers who were good at little else than praying to achieve rank among the first families of Shibboleth, Iowa. Once, in my salad days, I suggested to you such might have been the case. I don't believe that any more, but that interpretation's possible. Or, suppose your history were interpreted in political terms? In those early years, 1871 and after, the church was the center of a community's activity; here, I suspect, it's still as much a catalyst for political aspiration and action as was old North Church in Boston. In the eyes of the law you're a political entity—you're incorporated, you have a constitution entered on the commonwealth's books, and your documents are plumb full of those "whereases" as give a lawyer a cozy night's reading. With your growth your political "hold" on the community has increased, and I shouldn't wonder some envy you because they read your history in terms of pure, sheer political force.

If everything Paul did could be read in terms of mental imbalance; if the life of Luther could be construed as the result of an attack of constipation; if the Lord Jesus himself could be accused of being in league with the devil, who's to prevent your history's being viewed as aeons away from that loftier, nobler, higher thing you think it is? Part of the proof your history is hidden is that it's capable of a thousand and one interpretations.

And the other part is that what you've scratched and worked to build surrounds something, houses Someone you can't see. You've built to the glory of God—well, whoever in the world has seen him? You've erected altars from which to hand out the body and blood of Jesus Christ—now, where is he exactly? When my father talked to Sunday school children in his cassock and surplice, some little fellow whispered to the other: "Hey, there's God!" and when I first arrived here with my bride, it appeared you all felt the same about my predecessor, that with his going, the glory had departed from Israel! But boys and men soon learn "no one has ever seen God," no matter how some wonderful people come to reflect him.

Your history, your story as it meets the eye is like an onion—peel it away and what's left to see is air. Haven't there been those who refused to worship here, refused to confess what you confess, spurned your company, for whom everything you've planned and projected and established meant nothing, nothing at all; who believed it was all a Hans Christian Anderson tale of the emperor's clothes? And haven't you wondered whether that something, Someone you've never seen, and about whom you've carved one hundred years, three hundred sixty-five thousand days' history, may be only a will-o-the-wisp, an illusion? When you're sick or in despair, when love is gone, when meaning to life is lost, haven't you had second thoughts? You've never seen God, bless your heart, and that's the juiciest proof of all your history, your story is hidden.

Now why? Why should it be so? Why, when all is said and done, should all your life and force and energy boil down to what can't be seen, tasted, smelled or handled? Because of the cross of Jesus Christ! You've heard of it and what it's done a million times. In this letter, Paul writes that through it God reconciled to himself all things, whether on earth or in heaven; that he made peace by its blood; that by it God canceled the bond against us with its legal demands, set it aside, nailing it to the cross; that through it God disarmed the principalities and powers and made a public example of them, triumphing over them. For Paul there was little left to say once he'd pointed to that cross. Nothing left to say, really: "I decided to know *nothing* among you," he wrote elsewhere, "except Jesus Christ and him crucified."

You know. You've heard of that cross, prayed it, whispered it, sung it: "Jesus, crucified for me, Is my life, my hope's foundation, And my glory and salvation!" You know. But that doesn't make it any the less strange—I mean, that God should act in this way to bring the universe to heel; should reconcile all things in a monstrous alienation—Jesus cried: "Why hast thou forsaken me?"—should make peace in an hour of such hostility; should wring our freedom by a public execution; should triumph in an hour of defeat—"This is *your* hour," he said to his judges, "and the power of darkness." That's strange, and what it means is that God will not be where men expect him—in all those places where historians gather their stuff to write histories: in majesty, might and pomp, in the observable, provable, measurable and marketable.

God's love in the cross of Jesus forever marks his activity as hidden, concealed deep beneath what men can see, as the opposite to what men feel or think or want. God revealed himself, but in hiddenness. So, where others see nothing, there he is! and God bless every lonely soul for whom all he is and does, all he believes, all he wants is for nothing and who has strength left only to ache for him. Where others see tragedy, there he wins, and God bless every man who's made inventory of his life and seen there only defeat, but who's fastened what hope he has left on him. And, where others see something, everything, the whole world and heaven too, where they're pious and proud, ecstatic with their goodness, full of religion and up and doing, there he's not. God is hidden, hidden in Jesus, hidden in his cross, and because you belong to him, what you are, what you have done, is hidden there!

To let it be there, to let your history be hidden there—to allow, confess, to boast and brag that your life, your existence, everything about you has been plunged into one grand and unobservable thing with him, one grand hidden thing, that's your freedom. Freedom from men want to put a price tag on you, weigh you in the scales. Men can be terrible, frightful judges. God in his infinite love has allowed you what men call success, magnificent success! But suppose in his strange wisdom he should have kept you as you were in the late twenties and thirties, with hardly a sign of growth? You know what it meant, some of you, to suffer scorn and contempt in those days. Now, with the radical reversal of values, some might decide those days were your ripest, most golden—who knows? And there's the rub—who knows, when we leave the judgment to men? Who knows what decade in this history was best? Let it be hidden, your history—men judge by the legs of a man, the shape of a girl, size of the beef, kernel in the ear, by bank account and color of skin and party line—and they are frightful judges. But to leave the judgment to God, to God who will never be anything else for you than love, love without strings, love without conditions, who loves you not because he sees something in you others don't, but loves you for no earthly reason—that's a grand and glorious thing! To let it be hidden there, that life, that history of yours, there and nowhere else, in no one else, in nothing else, will make you an atheist of sorts, for there'll be no tie, no allegiance; there'll be no ideology, no interpretation to life, no aspiration, no dream, no native soil, no city, no place to grab you in your innards and make up the spring of your action. There'll be nothing left but a life hidden in God.

And it'll be a freedom to give what all can give. For look, if God veils himself under the sign of his opposite in that cross; if he spurns all that stuff that normally makes for history; if he won't have mighty deeds and weighty words and the gold of Croesus and the power of Rome, what then does he want, what can he get? What all can give, what no living, breathing man is without—faith, hope and love! So you've no wealth—well, neighbor, give God your heart; it's all he asks. So you've no power—well, hope in God. So you've no speech, no eloquence, no beauty—well, love your neighbor, it's all he needs! How strange and absurdly wonderful of God to arrange life and truth and existence in such fashion that in the end each can give what only *all* can give! How infinitely compassionate of God that he should plunge himself in hiddenness so that in the end no man can be what all cannot be—believers, lovers!

Life with Christ in God—there's your history. It's hidden, concealed, capable of a thousand and one interpretations; built around what can't be touched or measured—and because of a cross which hides everything in the nothing, turns truth to lie and lie to truth, death to life and weakness to power, and so frees us of any human judge; makes us free at last to give and see and hear and know. And all because of his love! God give you another hundred years, and a hundred more, and still another hundred to make such history!

Grow in Grace

But grow in the grace and knowledge of our Lord and
Savior Jesus Christ. To him be the glory both now and to
the day of eternity. Amen. (2 Peter 3:18)

My father—God rest his noble old bones—preached on this
text at my confirmation. I was an undersize thirteen, with more
hair than body, lost out in talent semi-finals to tap dancers and
got red marks in deportment at Ebinger School on Pratt Avenue.
I still remember, as though it were yesterday, the moment that
man who'd read me Mother Goose, crawled into my bed all
tobacco smoke and sweat and tickled me with his whiskers, went
berserk on the Fourth of July and in hardware stores, when he
looked me in the eye like the Almighty and asked: "Do you
renounce the devil and all his works and all his ways?"

A good bit of sentiment attaches to that old event for me, but
one, hard, bright truth shines through all the prunes and prisms,
and that's the announcement of the possibility of change, the
good news that what prevailed yesterday is not today's law, that
a man is not prey to some ineluctable fate, only half anticipated,
half gotten 'round with his horoscope, the gospel to fracture the
myth of blind chance in face of the new, the strange, the
unexpected.

Now, the day on which I first heard this word was a surfeit of
confidence; so there was the danger of interpreting it in terms of
the current philosophy—in terms of uninterrupted progress, evo-
lution, each new stage better than the last, in terms of that optimism from which no American ever seems to get free and which

110

when contradicted by events produces a divorce in the self—
optimism summed up in that old chestnut of Emil Coué: "Every
day in every way I'm getting better and better." Now that pretty
little theory of progress was never meant to be the house in
which this talk of growing should have its home! *That* was to
be the word that God's going to do a new and mighty thing, so
grow; God's going to melt heaven and earth, so change; God's
going to pour them like wax into the mould and out's going to
come the new home of justice, so become, develop, change and
grow! Jesus leaned, strained, yearned and grew to the tomorrow; He healed the sick and raised the dead—tore off a piece of
what was to come and set it in the here and now! "If I by the
finger of God cast out demons," he said, "then the kingdom of
God is come upon you!" It's not just a matter of "when you're
down and out. ..."

Now before you think you're being teased into jumping
through some Pollyanna hoop, into doing a big fat trick with
the self or the world on your own hook, remember what that
Second Peter—whoever in the world he was—says: The growing's
done in Christ, by grace! There's a good deal of palaver around
here about the prophetic—prophetic this, prophetic that. As
though a man sat down and decided to be prophetic, like decid-
ing for belts instead of suspenders. Prophetic, schmophetic! The
ancient prophet took his word and his power from *outside himself*—that's what those stories of the visions of Isaiah and Ezekiel
are meant to say. And the vanity that goes with all this chatter
about the prophetic has nothing to do with another thing
marked the genuine, grade A prophet of the Jews: *He forgot
himself!* That's what all those bizarre tales of the ecstasies of
Balaam and Saul are meant to say.

It's by grace, then, by the everlasting, unconditioned, unquali-
fied love and favor of God that the growing's done! It's his day

a-coming, his new world looming up, his promise, his patience given for amendment of life, his sovereignty, his kingdom, his glory! So grow, so yield the citadel of do-it-yourself—all that onward, upward, outward twaddle, all that "ought" and "must" and "should" business, all that legislating one another into communicating, celebrating, identifying, loving, changing—that old pap, that old con game that sowed the seeds of frustration which ripened into two world wars! It's not idealism, not law men need—bless my soul, it's the gospel, the good news of God's tomorrow coming on cat's feet, and the invitation, not the imperative but the invitation to grow into it; the promise, not the prerequisite but the promise that growth and change and the new are yours, waiting for you and free as air, by the grace, the favor, the unbelievable love of God! Grow, little brother, grow, and to him be the glory, Amen!